D0984373

WAR

OPPOSING VIEWPOINTS®

Other Books of Related Interest

OPPOSING VIEWPOINTS SERIES

Biological Warfare
Iraq
The Middle East
National Security
Terrorism
The War on Terrorism
Weapons of Mass Destruction

CURRENT CONTROVERSIES SERIES

Homeland Security
Iraq
The Middle East
The Terrorist Attack on America

AT ISSUE SERIES

Are Efforts to Reduce Terrorism Successful?
The Attack on America: September 11, 2001
Biological and Chemical Weapons
Do Nuclear Weapons Pose a Serious Threat?
Homeland Security
How Should the United States Withdraw from Iraq?
Islamic Fundamentalism
Is Military Action Justified Against Nations That Support Terrorism?
Is North Korea a Global Threat?
Missile Defense
National Security
The Peace Movement
U.S. Policy Toward Rogue Nations
What Motivates Suicide Bombers?

WAR

OPPOSING VIEWPOINTS®

Louise I. Gerdes, *Book Editor*

Bruce Glassman, *Vice President*
Bonnie Szumski, *Publisher*
Helen Cothran, *Managing Editor*

OPPOSING
VIEWPOINTS®
SERIES

GREENHAVEN PRESS
An imprint of Thomson Gale, a part of The Thomson Corporation

THOMSON
★
GALE

Detroit • New York • San Francisco • San Diego • New Haven, Conn.
Waterville, Maine • London • Munich

© 2005 Thomson Gale, a part of The Thomson Corporation.

Thomson and Star Logo are trademarks and Gale and Greenhaven Press are registered trademarks used herein under license.

For more information, contact
Greenhaven Press
27500 Drake Rd.
Farmington Hills, MI 48331-3535
Or you can visit our Internet site at http://www.gale.com

LIBRARY OF CONGRESS CATALOGING-IN-PUBLICATION DATA

War : opposing viewpoints / Louise I. Gerdes, book editor.
   p. cm. — (Opposing viewpoints series)
Includes bibliographical references and index.
ISBN 0-7377-2591-5 (lib. : alk. paper) — ISBN 0-7377-2592-3 (pbk. : alk. paper)
   1. Social conflict. 2. War. I. Gerdes, Louise I., 1953– . II. Opposing viewpoints
series (Unnumbered)
HM1121.W37 2005
303.6'6—dc22   2004054283

Printed in the United States of America

"Congress shall make no law. . . abridging the freedom of speech, or of the press."

First Amendment to the U.S. Constitution

The basic foundation of our democracy is the First Amendment guarantee of freedom of expression. The Opposing Viewpoints Series is dedicated to the concept of this basic freedom and the idea that it is more important to practice it than to enshrine it.

Contents

Why Consider Opposing Viewpoints?   9

Introduction   12

Chapter 1: What Causes War?

Chapter Preface   16

1. Religious Conflicts Cause War   18
   Daniel C. Tosteson

2. Religious Conflicts Do Not Cause War   23
   Vincent Carroll

3. Globalization Promotes War   28
   Steven Staples

4. Globalization Does Not Promote War   34
   Daniel T. Griswold

5. Capitalism Leads to War   38
   Green Party of Great Britain

6. Capitalism Does Not Lead to War   45
   Andrew Bernstein

7. Pacifism Escalates War   49
   Alex Epstein

8. Warlike Societies Perpetuate War   53
   Barbara Ehrenreich

Periodical Bibliography   58

Chapter 2: When Is War Justified?

Chapter Preface   60

1. War Is Sometimes Justified to Maintain Peace
   and Promote Freedom   62
   George Weigel

2. War Does Not Maintain Peace or Promote
   Freedom   71
   Wendell Berry

3. Preemptive War Is Sometimes Justified   80
   Michael J. Glennon

4. Preemptive War Cannot Be Justified   89
   Charles W. Kegley Jr. and Gregory A. Raymond

5. The War on Terror Is Justified 99
Institute for American Values

6. The War on Terror Is Not Justified 106
Tim Wise

Periodical Bibliography 113

Chapter 3: How Should War Be Conducted?

Chapter Preface 116

1. Detainees in the War on Terror Should Be
   Treated as Prisoners of War 118
   Bruce Shapiro

2. Detainees in the War on Terror Should Not
   Be Treated as Prisoners of War 124
   Ronald D. Rotunda

3. Civilians Should Not Be Targeted to Spare
   Combatants 128
   Brian Carnell

4. Civilians Should Sometimes Be Targeted to Spare
   Combatants 132
   Onkar Ghate

5. The United States Should Uphold Strict
   International Laws of War 136
   Michael Byers

6. The United States Should Reject Strict
   International Laws of War 146
   David B. Rivkin and Lee A. Casey

7. The United States Should Join the International
   Criminal Court to Pursue War Crimes 156
   Jonathan F. Fanton

8. The United States Should Not Join the International
   Criminal Court to Pursue War Crimes 160
   Ruth Wedgwood

Periodical Bibliography 171

Chapter 4: How Can War Be Prevented?

Chapter Preface 174

1. War Can Be Prevented 176
   Dane Spencer

2. War Cannot Be Prevented   182
   Victor Davis Hanson

3. Fostering Democracy Worldwide Will Prevent
   War   190
   R.J. Rummel

4. Peaceful Intervention Can Prevent War   200
   Friends Committee on National Legislation

5. Promoting Individual Liberty and Free Trade
   Will Avoid War   205
   Richard M. Ebeling

6. Letting Wars Run Their Course Leads to
   Lasting Peace   214
   Edward N. Luttwak

Periodical Bibliography   223

For Further Discussion   224
Organizations to Contact   227
Bibliography of Books   232
Index   234

Why Consider Opposing Viewpoints?

"The only way in which a human being can make some approach to knowing the whole of a subject is by hearing what can be said about it by persons of every variety of opinion and studying all modes in which it can be looked at by every character of mind. No wise man ever acquired his wisdom in any mode but this."

John Stuart Mill

In our media-intensive culture it is not difficult to find differing opinions. Thousands of newspapers and magazines and dozens of radio and television talk shows resound with differing points of view. The difficulty lies in deciding which opinion to agree with and which "experts" seem the most credible. The more inundated we become with differing opinions and claims, the more essential it is to hone critical reading and thinking skills to evaluate these ideas. Opposing Viewpoints books address this problem directly by presenting stimulating debates that can be used to enhance and teach these skills. The varied opinions contained in each book examine many different aspects of a single issue. While examining these conveniently edited opposing views, readers can develop critical thinking skills such as the ability to compare and contrast authors' credibility, facts, argumentation styles, use of persuasive techniques, and other stylistic tools. In short, the Opposing Viewpoints Series is an ideal way to attain the higher-level thinking and reading skills so essential in a culture of diverse and contradictory opinions.

In addition to providing a tool for critical thinking, Opposing Viewpoints books challenge readers to question their own strongly held opinions and assumptions. Most people form their opinions on the basis of upbringing, peer pressure, and personal, cultural, or professional bias. By reading carefully balanced opposing views, readers must directly confront new ideas as well as the opinions of those with whom they disagree. This is not to simplistically argue that everyone who reads opposing views will—or should— change his or her opinion. Instead, the series enhances readers' understanding of their own views by encouraging confrontation with opposing ideas. Careful examination of others' views can lead to the readers' understanding of the logical inconsistencies in their own opinions, perspective on why they hold an opinion, and the consideration of the possibility that their opinion requires further evaluation.

Evaluating Other Opinions

To ensure that this type of examination occurs, Opposing Viewpoints books present all types of opinions. Prominent spokespeople on different sides of each issue as well as well-known professionals from many disciplines challenge the reader. An additional goal of the series is to provide a forum for other, less known, or even unpopular viewpoints. The opinion of an ordinary person who has had to make the decision to cut off life support from a terminally ill relative, for example, may be just as valuable and provide just as much insight as a medical ethicist's professional opinion. The editors have two additional purposes in including these less known views. One, the editors encourage readers to respect others' opinions—even when not enhanced by professional credibility. It is only by reading or listening to and objectively evaluating others' ideas that one can determine whether they are worthy of consideration. Two, the inclusion of such viewpoints encourages the important critical thinking skill of objectively evaluating an author's credentials and bias. This evaluation will illuminate an author's reasons for taking a particular stance on an issue and will aid in readers' evaluation of the author's ideas.

It is our hope that these books will give readers a deeper understanding of the issues debated and an appreciation of the complexity of even seemingly simple issues when good and honest people disagree. This awareness is particularly important in a democratic society such as ours in which people enter into public debate to determine the common good. Those with whom one disagrees should not be regarded as enemies but rather as people whose views deserve careful examination and may shed light on one's own.

Thomas Jefferson once said that "difference of opinion leads to inquiry, and inquiry to truth." Jefferson, a broadly educated man, argued that "if a nation expects to be ignorant and free . . . it expects what never was and never will be." As individuals and as a nation, it is imperative that we consider the opinions of others and examine them with skill and discernment. The Opposing Viewpoints Series is intended to help readers achieve this goal.

David L. Bender and Bruno Leone,
Founders

Greenhaven Press anthologies primarily consist of previously published material taken from a variety of sources, including periodicals, books, scholarly journals, newspapers, government documents, and position papers from private and public organizations. These original sources are often edited for length and to ensure their accessibility for a young adult audience. The anthology editors also change the original titles of these works in order to clearly present the main thesis of each viewpoint and to explicitly indicate the opinion presented in the viewpoint. These alterations are made in consideration of both the reading and comprehension levels of a young adult audience. Every effort is made to ensure that Greenhaven Press accurately reflects the original intent of the authors included in this anthology.

Introduction

"War destroys, it does not create. It is not destruction, but reconstuction that can give hope for the future."
—*Jonathan Lash, President, World Resources Institute*

American Civil War general William Tecumseh Sherman advised the graduating cadets at Michigan Military Academy in 1879, "You don't know the horrible aspects of war. I've been through two wars and I know. I've seen cities and homes in ashes. I've seen thousands of men lying on the ground, their dead faces looking up at the skies. I tell you, war is hell!" Historical commentary is replete with details of war's tragic consequences: lives lost, cities ruined, economies drained, and vast populations displaced. War's devastating impact on the environment, however, has often been ignored. That has begun to change with the advent of modern warfare.

After Iraq invaded its neighbor Kuwait in 1990, the United Nations sent coalition forces to liberate Kuwait in what is known as the Gulf War. In early 1991, as UN forces advanced, Iraqi president Saddam Hussein retaliated by ordering Iraqi forces to deliberately dump an estimated 11 million barrels of oil into the Persian Gulf, killing more than thirty thousand marine birds, contaminating more than 20 percent of the surrounding mangroves, and killing over 50 percent of the nearby coral reefs. Iraqi troops also stayed behind in Kuwait long enough to set fire to more than 730 oil wells. The burning wells emitted soot into the air, changing the local climate and contributing to acid rain. Upon touring Kuwait's burnt-out oil fields, one scientist remarked on the Peace Pledge Union Web site:

> I've never seen such devastation. Kuwait's desert before the Gulf War was very healthy, despite centuries of nomadic grazing and decades of oil development. It supported substantial greenery and wildlife. But now it's coated in oil residues that affect water permeability, seed germination and microbial life. Plants are dying because they can't breathe through blackened leaves under dark skies.

Although war has always had a destructive impact on the environment, some commentators argue that modern warfare may cause irrevocable environmental damage. International law scholar Claire Inder claims, "It is undeniable that modern weapons systems now have the capacity to destroy the planet many times over and the potential damage this technology could have on the environment in any armed conflict is far greater than ever." For example, Inder explains that the conventional weapons used against Iraq in 1991 were equivalent to ten nuclear bombs.

Although the destruction of the environment by Iraqi forces in Kuwait was a retaliatory strategy designed to leave Kuwait in ruins, often the environment in war-torn regions is deliberately harmed to gain military advantage. The Romans destroyed their enemies' crops to ensure that upon defeat their enemies would become dependent on Rome. In 1812 Russians employed a scorch-and-burn policy to deprive Napoléon's troops of food, shelter, and warmth. It was not until the devastating herbicidal deforestation of Vietnam, however, that policy makers added environmental protection to the international laws of war.

During the Vietnam War (1964–1973), the U.S. military carried out a massive herbicidal deforestation program in South Vietnam. U.S. and South Vietnamese forces sprayed 72 million liters of chemicals to defoliate forests that provided cover for Communist guerrillas. One herbicide, Agent Orange, has since been indirectly linked with cancer, birth defects, and miscarriages. South Vietnamese civilians and U.S. veterans still have high levels of the chemical's components in their bloodstreams, and their children, born more than thirty years after the war, also show signs of contamination. In addition, 40 percent of Vietnam's forests still show defoliant damage. "All of our coconut trees died," recalls a Vietnamese woman on the Peace Pledge Union Web site. "Some of our animals died, and those that lived had deformed offspring. The seeds of the rice became very small, and we couldn't use them for replanting."

The devastating impact of this military strategy on the environment and its human and animal inhabitants motivated concerned policy makers to develop international laws that specifically protect the environment in times of war. In 1977 Protocol I was added to the 1949 Geneva Convention, an international agreement first formulated in Geneva, Switzer-land, in 1864, which establishes wartime rules for the treat-ment of civilians, the wounded, and prisoners of war. Article 55 of the 1977 Protocol states, "Care shall be taken in warfare to protect the natural environment against widespread, long-term, and severe damage." In addition, the Environmental Modification Convention (ENMOD) was created to forbid the "military or any other hostile use of environmental modi-fication techniques having widespread, long-lasting or severe effects as the means of destruction, damage or injury to any other State Party." The treaty defined environmental modifi-cation techniques as "any technique for changing—through the deliberate manipulation of natural processes—the dynam-ics, composition or structure of the Earth, including its biota, lithosphere, hydrosphere and atmosphere, or of outer space."

However, environmental activists contend that Protocol I and ENMOD are insufficient to protect the environment against the devastation of modern warfare. The terms of these agreements, they argue, are ambiguous. For example, the definitions of "widespread," "long-term," and "severe" are unclear and thus difficult to enforce. Inder maintains, "Unless the international community is able to formulate more specific protection and regulation than is currently of-fered, the damage to the environment in armed conflict will only continue to worsen, with unforeseeable consequences."

Whether treaties or international laws governing the con-duct of war can effectively limit the environmental devastation of war remains controversial. Other debates concerning war are presented in the following chapters of *Opposing Viewpoints: War:* What Causes War? When Is War Justified? How Should War Be Conducted? How Can War Be Prevented? Environmental activists express concern over what they be-lieve to be an increasingly serious consequence of war. Ac-cording to Inder, "Without the determination of unambigu-ous international protection of the environment in times of war, then in the future States may have to face a new, common enemy of far greater threat to national security than any other state has ever been—that of environmental degradation."

CHAPTER 1

What Causes War?

Chapter Preface

American writer Mark Twain is claimed to have said, "In the West, whiskey's for drinking, and water's for fighting over." At the turn of the twentieth century, the American Southwest was not unlike many nations today—prone to drought. Although dams and other technologies have helped ameliorate water problems in the American Southwest and other dry regions around the world, water problems persist as supplies continue to diminish worldwide. Some of the world's mightiest rivers—the Nile in Africa, the Yellow in Asia, the Colorado in the United States, and the Murray in Australia—no longer reach the sea. Despite existing dams, pipes, canals, and levees, one in five people worldwide lacks access to safe drinking water. According to public health journalist Mark Townsend, "An acute scarcity of drinking water fuelled by massive population growth means that, in as little as 14 years, almost half the world's people will live in countries drastically short of this most vital resource." Some analysts predict that disputes over increasingly scarce water supplies will lead to war. Others assert that water wars are not inevitable; in fact, they claim, water is a catalyst for peace.

Many commentators argue that water scarcity is cause for war. At a 2002 international security conference, scientists and experts from the Royal United Services Institute for Defence Studies (RUSI) warned that in Africa, the Middle East, northern China, and much of Asia, a shortage of water could lead to instability and ultimately war. RUSI experts cite, for example, efforts by Sudan and Ethiopia to interfere with the headwaters of the Nile to satisfy their own needs. Townsend reports that such efforts "could cripple Egypt—whose population of 68 million is projected to reach 97 million by 2025—and which relies almost solely on the river for its [water] supply." Andrew Kennedy, head of Southeast Asian Security for RUSI, claims, "We are seeing conflicts surrounding water-tables in the Middle East. Water is such a vital resource that attacking dams and poisoning water supplies is a major potential weapon."

Kader Asmal, South Africa's Minister of Education and member of the World Water Commission, disagrees with these dire predictions. He contends that there is no evidence to back up the theory that water scarcity will lead to war. "It is true that stress, tensions and disputes are inevitable, in and between nations," says Asmal. "Water, or even sediment, used or diverted by you, upstream, is not available for me, struggling downstream. I am likely to get 'tight jaws' over your plans to develop it." Nevertheless, Asmal argues, history proves that wars over water are not inevitable. "I have seen sovereign states and ethnic groups within nations go to war over every resource—oil, land, humans, diamonds, gas, livestock, or gold—but never, interestingly, over renewable resources, and never, in particular, over water development and dams."

Analysts such as Asmal argue that water disputes in fact tend to force countries to cooperate rather than go to war. "Indeed, just as rain does not start but rather cools and suppresses fire," Asmal maintains, "so water, by its very nature, tends to induce even hostile co-riparian countries to cooperate. . . . The weight of historical evidence demonstrates that organized political bodies have signed 3600 water related treaties since AD 805." Asmal concludes, "Twain was exactly wrong. We may step outside to decide what to do about scarcity of whiskey. But as for water, it was never in the past, is not now and will not be in the future—for fighting over. Water is for conserving. Water is for bathing. Water is for drinking. Water is for sharing. Water is the catalyst for peace."

Whether water scarcity will lead to war remains the subject of heated debate. The authors in the following chapter explore other factors that cause people to go to war.

"A particularly salient recurrent cause of the plague of war is conflicting religious convictions."

Religious Conflicts Cause War

Daniel C. Tosteson

Disagreements over religious convictions are a common cause of war, argues Daniel C. Tosteson in the following viewpoint. As technology makes encounters between people with diverse religious views more frequent, he maintains, the plague of war will spread. Since people are not likely to abandon religion, the best way to resolve religious conflict is to adapt a global principle of separation of church and state and a worldview that tolerates religious diversity, Tosteson claims. Tosteson, a professor of cell biology, is former president of the American Academy of Arts and Sciences.

As you read, consider the following questions:
1. According to Tosteson, what has the human mind continued to breed in addition to discoveries in biomedical science?
2. From what does the deep human passion for hegemony arise, in the author's view?
3. In the author's opinion, why is it unlikely that humans will renounce religion altogether?

Daniel C. Tosteson, "Unhealthy Beliefs: Religion and the Plague of War," *Daedalus*, vol. 132, Summer 2003, p. 80. Copyright © 2003 by the American Academy of Arts and Sciences. Reproduced by permission of *Daedalus*: Journal of the American Academy of Arts and Sciences.

In response to the savage terrorist attack on the World Trade Center in New York City and the Pentagon in Washington [on September 11, 2001], my country has resolved to wage the first war of the third millennium. The terrorist attack unjustly murdered thousands of human beings. In retaliation, many thousands more will die prematurely, infected by the lethal plague of war.

Unlike many infectious diseases, the plague of war is not caused by some virus or bacterium or parasite, but rather by a pathogen that is even more potentially lethal: the beliefs created by the human mind.

The Power of the Human Mind

Of course, the mind is responsible for the remarkable improvement in human health that has occurred during the last two centuries and, particularly, during the most recent few decades. Through the patient and careful observations and reasoning of many generations of scientists and scholars, we have learned to recognize the microbial origins of many infectious diseases and discovered ways of preventing and curing many of them. In this sense, the human mind is our most powerful resource for protection against illness. The recent emergence of SARS [Severe Acute Respiratory Syndrome] and the recognition that it is caused by a hitherto undescribed mutant of coronavirus reminds us of our increasing skill in managing our endless competition with pathogenic microbes.

Still, for all the remarkable discoveries wrought by biomedical science, the human mind continues to breed murderous convictions. It has proved infinitely ingenious in creating ever more deadly weapons of war: clubs, swords, arrows, lances, shells, biological and chemical poisons, conventional and nuclear explosives delivered by airplanes or guided missiles or minivans. And, given its ingenuity, attempts to reduce or eliminate war by preventing any particular mechanism of murder are unlikely to succeed, since other options for killing are, sooner or later, always invented.

The necessary and sufficient conditions for outbreaks of the plague of wars of terror are mutual hatred between two or more groups of people and the suspension of civil constraints against murder—indeed, the official glorification of mass murder that occurs during wartime. Many factors contribute to the development of these conditions: poverty, starvation, persecution, slavery, revenge, envy, greed, an insatiable desire for power—to name only a few.

Conflicting Religious Beliefs

But a particularly salient recurrent cause of the plague of war is conflicting religious convictions.

Often, the murderers are self-righteous in their belief that they are acting according to the will of the god or gods in whom they believe. By acts of persuasion or coercion or, as a last resort, by killing those who continue to disagree, they aim to bring all human beings into agreement with their beliefs. Their deep passion for hegemony arises partly from the desire to control the behavior of the infidels, and partly to avoid the confusion and anxiety aroused by the awareness that different groups of people may hold radically different religious beliefs.

The Religious Animal

Learned people always have known that faith has a potential for horror. Mark Twain wrote: "Man is the religious animal. . . . He is the only animal who has the true religion—several of them. He is the only animal who loves his neighbor as himself and cuts his throat, if his theology isn't straight. He has made a graveyard of the globe in trying his honest best to smooth his brother's path to happiness and heaven."

James A. Haught, *Liberty*, March/April 1996.

In the past, geographic isolation curbed the frequency and intensity of plagues of war between groups of human beings with conflicting belief systems. But modern technology has enabled the rapid transport of people and information, radically intensifying the encounters between peoples with conflicting convictions. Globalization accelerates not only the spread of infectious diseases caused by microbes, but also the plagues of war caused by incompatible religious convictions.

As the globalization of all human activities continues inexorably, as I believe it will, despite the protests of many disadvantaged and resentful citizens of the planet, the mutual hatred of groups of people with conflicting concepts of god will intensify and increase the probability of wars of terror.

The Possibility of a Secular Vision

What can the great majority of people who seek a peaceful life do to prevent or remedy the plague of unconditional hatred that infects the small minority who wage wars of terror?

It is easy to understand why some would choose to discourage religious belief altogether. It is not unreasonable to infer from the historical record that the price in human misery of wars between peoples with conflicting conceptions of god is too high.

Perhaps, at last, we could acknowledge that god is not the creator but a creature of the brain, a fiction that is useful for maintaining the fabric of a society that persists beyond the span of our individual lives. Perhaps we could accept and celebrate our individual deaths as an essential component in the vast system of living creatures of which we are a part. Perhaps we could elaborate a secular vision of the human situation that all might embrace, a vision that could sustain a healthy society without recourse to the outworn myths of our childhood. Perhaps we could all have the vision and courage to sing with the American poetess, Emily Dickinson, that, despite the inevitability of death, this life that we have, with all of its complexities, confusions, and hopes, is enough:

I reckon—when I count at all—
First—Poets—Then the Sun—
Then Summer—Then the Heaven of God—
And then—the List is done—

But, looking back—the First so seems
To Comprehend the Whole—
The Others look a needless Show . . .

But it is very unlikely that mankind will renounce religion altogether. Again drawing evidence from the historical record, the penchant to conceive a god or gods to account for our experiences, and, particularly, our personal deaths, is evident in almost all human societies. For this reason, we would do well to celebrate the capacity to discover (or invent) god as an essential step toward constructing a personal identity that allows us to respect and honor ourselves and our fellow human beings, but if we do so, we should also realize that differences of religious conviction are both likely and essential for learning—not expressions of disrespect.

But if all individuals are free to choose their own system of religious belief, then the possibility, even probability, of passionate conflict will persist. How then to inhibit the emergence of the unconditional hatred and suspension of civil constraints that produce the plagues of war?

A New Worldview

We must recognize that our all-too-human propensity to resort to violence is a form of mental illness, related to but even more dangerous than addiction to mind-altering drugs. Recent research on the neurobiological basis of warlike behavior reveals many paths worthy of exploration. But such research also suggests that the aggressive impulses of human beings, like the microbial infections that plague them, are unlikely to disappear anytime soon.

In the meantime, the best remedy is the global adoption of the principle of the separation of church and state, and the primacy of secular over sacred law. This will require the formulation, articulation, and adoption of a worldview that all of the earth's diverse citizens can embrace. We must search for new ways of thinking and feeling about ourselves and our fellow human beings that will lead toward a form of tolerance that is more mutually respectful and more accommodating to diversities of belief than anything we have yet achieved.

The need is urgent—for the failure to find a way could be catastrophic for life on earth.

"*Most of the important opponents of war,
persecution, oppression, and slavery in the
history of the West have also been driven
by religious conviction.*"

Religious Conflicts Do Not
Cause War

Vincent Carroll

According to Vincent Carroll in the following viewpoint,
claims that religion causes war are misleading. What some
contend to be religious wars, Carroll argues, were in reality
fought for secular reasons, including the desire for conquest,
a fear of scarce resources, and the rejection of central or foreign power. Mass killing resulting from secular motives re-
futes the theory that religion is the primary cause of war, Carroll maintains. Vincent Carroll, editor of the *Rocky Mountain
News*, is coauthor, with Dave Shiflett, of *Christianity on Trial:
Arguments Against Anti-Religious Bigotry*.

As you read, consider the following questions:
1. In Carroll's opinion, what individuals have historically
   sought to suppress private violence and impose rules on
   the conduct of war?
2. What did one war study of 186 societies find?
3. What examples does the author cite as evidence that the
   brutality of ethnic rivalry appears unrelated to religious
   differences?

"**R**eligious fanatics are the worst fanatics," the critic Garry Wills once declared, and who would want to argue after the [terrorist attacks] of Sept. 11 [2001]? Yet is it really true? Are zealots motivated by religious belief more absolutist, intolerant, and, yes, violent than zealots motivated by nonreligious aims?

Is the biologist Richard Dawkins correct when he denounces religion because it "causes wars"? Does it even cause "most wars," as Paul Harvey asserted in a 1998 broadcast?

The Conventional Wisdom

Such sentiments are virtually conventional wisdom in America, and they will become even more deeply entrenched given the facile pronouncements [in the weeks following the terrorist attacks]. One TV network's expert analyst, a former federal agent, marveled at the hijackers' capacity to live in this country for many months and not be seduced by middle-class materialism. Only a singular sort of indoctrination could produce such automatons, he suggested, the long-term treachery of Communist moles somehow having escaped his attention.

It so happens, of course, that religious enthusiasm probably does cause wars. And it probably also prevents them. Or at least that has been the case with Christianity, which itself is often accused of the same sort of fanaticism that brought down the World Trade Center.

"More people have been killed in the name of Jesus Christ than any other name in the history of the world," maintains [writer] Gore Vidal. Such anti-Christian bigots usually have in mind the religious wars of the 16th and 17th centuries—and of course the Crusades. These are fat targets, to be sure, although perhaps not quite so fat as many of those who cite them imagine.

Reexamining History

For one thing, even at the height of the post-Reformation bloodletting between Catholics and Protestants, secular motives were everywhere at play, and often held the upper hand. They involved rival rulers contending for power, local leaders resisting central government or a foreign state, and one class or region pitting itself against another. The suppression of the Irish under Oliver Cromwell, for example, looks a lot like a religious war from one perspective. From another, it looks like nothing so much as an old-fashioned imperial conquest in which the natives are dispossessed and massacred while the victors seize the spoils.

This is not to discount a genuine religious factor even in some of the worst atrocities. Pope Gregory XIII was so impressed by the Saint Bartholomew's Day Massacre of French Huguenots by Catholic mobs in 1572, for example, that he actually commissioned a commemorative medal. Religious sentiment was perhaps even more prominent in the Crusades—although it is usually forgotten, as [author] Piers Paul Read has pointed out, that "the Christians' perception was that wars against Islam were waged either in defense of Christendom or to liberate and reconquer lands that were rightfully theirs." Still, there is no getting around the fact that Pope Urban II galvanized the church's first holy war with his speech at Clermont in 1095, that St. Bernard exhorted the faithful to join the Second Crusade some half century later, and that popes such as Gregory VIII and Innocent III drummed up combatants for subsequent campaigns. There is equally no doubt that the ensuing slaughter could be breathtaking—and that the Crusades involved, in the words of the historian Stephen Neill, "a lowering of the whole moral temperature of Christendom."

A Misleading Label

The catalog of Christian aggression includes many entries besides these highlights, of course. Some are well-known abominations, such as the Inquisition; others have been widely forgotten, such as the forced conversion of the Saxons in the Eighth Century. Yet there are at least four reasons why it is nonetheless reckless and misleading to label Christianity a warmongering faith.

The first is that most of the important opponents of war, persecution, oppression, and slavery in the history of the West have also been driven by religious conviction. It was churchmen, after all, who often restrained the worst instincts of the converted barbarian kings, counseling mercy where none had been known. It was mainly church officials who sought to suppress private violence and impose rules on the conduct of war. And it was church canon law, reinforced by the code of chivalry, that provided the basis for a right of immunity for noncombatants.

The True Source of Conflict

Religious conflict tells us less about religion and more about human nature. Humans are capable of turning on each other for all kinds of reasons: historical, racial, cultural and personal as well as religious. In fact some of the worst atrocities committed within the [twentieth] century were carried out under régimes hostile to religion in the name of national and international socialism. In general, humans will fight about anything they feel strongly about from politics to carparking spaces.

Holy Trinity of Doncaster, www.holytrinitydoncaster.org.au, 2004.

Even the original Christian ethic of total nonviolence—"Put your sword back into its place; for all who take the sword will perish by the sword" (Matt. 26:52)—survived and was carried forward through the centuries: here by Catholic monks, there by Anabaptists, Mennonites, Moravians, Quakers, Dukhobors, Brethren, and many others. It was religious agitation that convinced the British government to grant exemption to military service for reasons of conscience as early as 1802. And, as secular governments embarked on imperial adventures that eventually circled the globe, it was men and women expressing their Christian conscience that decried the often-naked exploitation of these enterprises.

"The Christian acceptance of warfare was always somewhat conditional," observes historian James Turner Johnson. "The use of force was justified only if it was undertaken against evil, and the soldier was enjoined to hate the sin against which he was fighting, not the sinner."

The Actual Roots of War

The second reason is one well known to anthropologists: The vast majority of societies everywhere have engaged in warfare, and many have done so on a continual basis. One study of 186 societies found war "rare or absent" in only nine percent of them. The most common reason for conflict? Not religion, but fear of shortages or impending natural disaster.

The third reason is that other ideologies wedded to state power, including nationalism, seem equally ferocious with or without a religious component. Even the brutality of ethnic rivalry often appears unrelated to religious differences. The worst explosion of violence in modern Africa, for example—in Rwanda—occurred without the goad of religious animosity. And where religious difference does seem to heighten ethnic conflict—in Sudan, for example—it is difficult to believe that the clashing groups would have been holding hands had they shared the same faith. After all, as the British sociologist David Martin has observed: "Turks, Iraqis, and Iranians can slaughter Kurds, and vice versa, with an enthusiasm entirely unaltered by the presence or absence of religious difference. In Turkey Turks are largely Sunni, Kurds often Alawite. In Iraq Kurds are Sunni, like most Iraqis, and in Iran they are Sunni and the Iranians mostly Shia. But the degree of conflict remains fairly constant."

Secular Barbarism

The final reason is as obvious as it is irrefutable: Religious zealots have not in fact been the biggest butchers in Western history, or even close to it. The body count of corpses from the two great secular barbarisms of the 20th century, Communism and Nazism—both of which were hostile to the religions in their midst—runs to well over 100 million.

"For the historian of the year 3000, where will fanaticism lie? Where, the oppression of man by man? In the thirteenth century or the twentieth?," [author] Regine Pernoud aptly wondered a quarter of a century ago.

Each religion is a separate story, admittedly, and the motives at play throughout the history of Islamic jihad [holy war] have been notoriously difficult to disentangle. Yet even suicide terrorists, seemingly so foreign to the West, are not exactly unknown, even in the American heartland. Eric Harris and Dylan Klebold strode into Columbine High School [and killed twelve students and one teacher on April 20, 1999] knowing full well it was their final act, and neither cared a fig about religious faith.

| *"Globalization promotes the conditions that lead to unrest, inequality, conflict, and, ultimately, war."*

Globalization Promotes War

Steven Staples

In the following viewpoint Steven Staples argues that globalization promotes war because it creates the conditions that lead to war and encourages militarism. According to Staples, the corporate elite of affluent countries exploit the labor and resources of Third World nations, creating global economic inequality and competition for diminishing resources, the root causes of war. Moreover, he claims, globalization encourages these impoverished nations to spend minimal resources on expensive militaries to protect the interests of international corporations, providing these nations with the tools of war. Staples is chairman of the International Network on Disarmament and Globalization, a network of antiglobalization activists.

As you read, consider the following questions:
1. According to Staples, how does the mainstream media oversimplify the causes of wars?
2. In the author's view, how does the World Trade Organization promote military economies?
3. What example does the author use to support his argument that military supremacy has always been a prerequisite for economic integration into a sphere of influence or an empire?

G lobalization and militarism should be seen as two sides of the same coin. On one side, globalization promotes the conditions that lead to unrest, inequality, conflict, and, ultimately, war. On the other side, globalization fuels the means to wage war by protecting and promoting the military industries needed to produce sophisticated weaponry. This weaponry, in turn, is used—or its use is threatened—to protect the investments of transnational corporations and their shareholders.

Promoting Inequality, Unrest, and Conflict

Economic inequality is growing; more conflict and civil wars are emerging. It is important to see a connection between these two situations.

Proponents of global economic integration argue that globalization promotes peace and economic development of the Third World. They assert that "all boats rise with the tide" when investors and corporations make higher profits. However, there is precious little evidence that this is true and substantial evidence of the opposite.

The [1999] United Nations' Human Development Report noted that globalization is creating new threats to human security. Economic inequality between Northern and Southern nations has worsened, not improved. There are more wars being fought today—mostly in the Third World—than there were during the Cold War. Most are not wars between countries, but are civil wars where the majority of deaths are civilians, not soldiers.

The mainstream media frequently oversimplify the causes of these wars, with claims they are rooted in religious or ethnic differences. A closer inspection reveals that the underlying source of such conflicts is economic in nature. Financial instability, economic inequality, competition for resources, and environmental degradation—all root causes of war—are exacerbated by globalization.

The Asian financial meltdown of 1997 to 1999 involved a terrible human cost. The economies of Thailand, South Korea, and Indonesia crumbled in the crisis. These countries, previously held up by neoliberal economists as the darlings of globalization, were reduced to riots and financial ruin.

The International Monetary Fund (IMF) stepped in to rescue foreign investors and impose austerity programs that opened the way for an invasion by foreign corporations that bought up assets devalued by capital flight and threw millions of people out of work. Political upheaval and conflict ensued, costing thousands of lives.

Meanwhile, other countries watched as their neighbors suffered the consequences of greater global integration. In India, citizens faced corporate recolonization, which spawned a nationalistic political movement. Part of the political program was the development of nuclear weapons—seen by many as the internationally accepted currency of power. Nuclear tests have put an already conflict-ridden region on the brink of nuclear war.

Fueling the Means to Wage War

The world economic system promotes military economies over civilian economies, pushing national economic policies toward military spending. The World Trade Organization (WTO), one of the main instruments of globalization, is largely based on the premise that the only legitimate role for a government is to provide for a military to protect the interests of the country and a police force to ensure order within. The WTO attacks governments' social and environmental policies that reduce corporate profits, and it has succeeded in having national laws that protect the environment struck down. Yet the WTO gives exemplary protection to government actions that develop, arm, and deploy armed forces and supply a military establishment. Article XXI of the General Agreement on Tariffs and Trade (GATT) allows governments free rein for actions taken in the interest of national security.

For example, in 1999 a WTO trade panel ruled against a Canadian government program that provided subsidies to aerospace and defense corporations for the production of civilian aircraft. Within weeks, the Canadian military announced a new $30 million subsidy program for the same Canadian corporations, but this time the money was for production of new weapons. In this case, the government was forced down the path of a military economy.

Contrast this WTO ruling with the billions of dollars the Pentagon gives to American weapons corporations for developing and producing military aircraft. The $309-billion U.S. military budget dwarfs the budgets of all its potential enemies combined, and with the collapse of the Soviet Union the U.S. faces no imminent military challengers. This large budget is, for all practical purposes, a corporate subsidy. Because the corporations involved happen to be building weapons, the subsidy is protected under GATT's Article XXI.

The Violence of Globalization

Corporate globalization (Global Neoliberal Capitalism) is a form of economic coercion designed to wrest control of natural resources away from resident populations (mainly poor indigenous peoples and people of color primarily in the Global South). This economic coercion is likewise used to transform even human beings into expendable resources.

Communities that attempt to resist this economic violence are met with military violence at the hands of paramilitaries, police and armies. These forms of violence are two sides of the same corporate globalization coin.

Global Justice Ecology Project, "Corporate Globalization, War, and the Environment: It's All One Struggle," March 30, 2004.

The use of military spending to develop a country's industrial and economic base has not been lost on Third World countries. Though struggling to lift itself from apartheid-era poverty and accompanying social problems, South Africa is spending billions of dollars on aircraft, warships, and even submarines in an effort to develop its economy.

South Africa stipulated that the arms it buys must be partially manufactured in South Africa. Finance Minister Trevor Manuel explained that the increase in military spending would allow "the National Defence Force to upgrade equipment, while providing a substantial boost to South African industry, foreign investment, and exports." South Africa's performance requirements would be wide open to WTO challenges if they were for building schools, hospitals, transportation infrastructure, or virtually anything except weapons.

South Africa is about to make the same mistake Northern industrialized countries made: it is creating new military projects that will become dependent on perpetual government funding, drawing money away from essential social programs. When the current weapons orders have been filled and government funding dries up, weapons corporations will have to find new customers to maintain current job levels, driving the arms trade and potentially causing a whole new arms race in the region. . . .

Using Force to Protect Corporate Interests

According to *New York Times* columnist Thomas Friedman, "the hidden hand of the market will never work without a hidden fist. McDonald's cannot flourish without McDonnell Douglas, the builder of the F-15. And the hidden fist that keeps the world safe for Silicon Valley's technologies is called the United States Army, Air Force, Navy, and Marine Corps."

Friedman illuminates the strategic relationship that exists between corporations and militaries. As globalization extends the reach of corporate interests around the world, a matching military capacity must be deployed to protect those interests. This is the underlying reason the U.S. military maintains the capacity to wage two major wars in different regions of the world simultaneously.

There is nothing new about Friedman's "hidden fist." Military supremacy has always been a prerequisite for economic integration into a sphere of influence or an empire. One can see this in the settling of the New World, when the network of military forts and outposts suppressed First Nations peoples and opened North America for settlers, prospectors, and industry barons.

Outer space is the next frontier to be made safe for corporations, according to U.S. military strategists. In Vision for 2020, the U.S. Space Command revealed that the "U.S. Space Command [is] dominating the space dimensions of military operations to protect U.S. interests and investment."

Globalization is driving a global war economy and creating the conditions for tremendous loss of human life. Many writers and researchers have documented the decline in human rights, social justice, environmental standards, and democracy caused by globalization. The inevitable outcome of globalization will be more wars—especially in the Third World where globalization has its harshest effects. Meanwhile, the elites of the industrialized world are confident that the global economy will continue to provide them with wealth created from the resources and labor of the Third World. Their technologically advanced militaries will protect them and their investments, insulating them from the violent effects of globalization.

What is required is a complete reassessment of the current global economic system, with the goal of promoting genuine human security and development. Global financial institutions, such as the World Trade Organization, that do not promote these goals must be revised or scrapped completely and replaced with a system based upon principles of equity, peace, and democracy.

"There is no evidence that globalization has fomented violence, either within or among countries."

Globalization Does Not Promote War

Daniel T. Griswold

According to Daniel T. Griswold in the following viewpoint, globalization reduces conflict. Globalization helps people achieve higher incomes and more education, which in turn promotes political and civil liberties, argues Griswold. These developments result in fewer wars, he asserts, because democracies are less likely to fight with each other. Closed economies, on the other hand, promote political tyranny and poverty, which lead to war, he asserts. Griswold is associate director of the Center for Trade Policy Studies at the Cato Institute, a conservative public policy think tank.

As you read, consider the following questions:

1. In Griswold's view, what has occurred in developing countries that have aggressively opened their economies?
2. According to the author, what has happened to the world's population in the past thirty years, as globalization has gained momentum?
3. Why has the incidence of civil war declined in developing nations embracing globalization but risen in Africa, in the author's opinion?

Daniel T. Griswold, "The Best Way to Grow Future Democracies," *Philadelphia Inquirer*, February 15, 2004. Copyright © 2004 by the *Philadelphia Inquirer* and the Cato Institute. Reproduced by permission.

P eople who live in countries open to the global economy
enjoy a higher standard of living, on average, than those
trapped behind high-tariff barriers. They eat better and live
longer. Their children are more likely to attend school than
work in the fields. They can speak, assemble and worship
more freely and elect their rulers democratically. And because economically open countries are more likely to be
democracies, they are less likely to fight wars with each other.

The Benefits of Open Societies

Those observations are based not on academic theories, but
on how the world really works. Study after study confirms
that nations open to international commerce grow faster and
achieve higher incomes than those that are closed. That's because open societies can more readily specialize in what they
do best, and take advantage of lower global prices to benefit
families and producers alike. As a result, the most dramatic
progress against poverty has occurred in developing countries that have most aggressively opened their economies,
such as China, Vietnam, Uganda, Chile and India.

Higher incomes mean a larger, more educated and politically engaged middle class—the foundation of most democracies. In a . . . study for the Cato Institute [a public policy
think tank], I found that citizens of nations that are the most
open to trade are three times more likely to enjoy full political and civil liberties than those in nations that are the most
closed to trade. Those in economically closed nations are
nine times more likely to suffer under political tyranny than
those in open economies.

In the past 30 years, as globalization has gained momentum, the share of the world's population that enjoys full political and civil freedoms has increased from 35 to 44 percent, while the share deprived of such freedoms fell from 47
to 35 percent. (The share in partly free countries rose from
18 to 21 percent.) The number of democracies worldwide
has risen sharply in the past 15 years along with the spread
of more liberal and open economic policies.

There is no evidence that globalization has fomented violence, either within or among countries. The worst ethnic
strife in recent years has occurred in relatively protected and

Economic Freedom and Per Capita Income

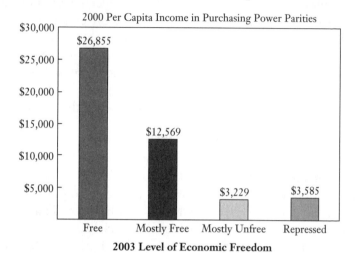

2000 Per Capita Income in Purchasing Power Parities

2003 Level of Economic Freedom

World Bank, *World Development Indicators on CD-ROM 2002*; Central Intelligence Agency, *The World Factbook 2001*; The Heritage Foundation and *The Wall Street Journal*, the *2003 Index of Economic Freedom*.

undemocratic societies such as Rwanda, Sierra Leone, Zimbabwe, and the former Yugoslavia. Envy and violence against economically successful ethnic minorities long predate globalization.

Globalization Promotes Peace

If anything, globalization has put a damper on such conflicts. A recent World Bank study concluded: "The incidence of civil war has declined sharply in the globalizing developing regions, but has risen sharply in Africa."

The reason is straightforward: Expanding markets channel a people's ambition and energy into creating wealth, while closed and stagnant markets breed frustration and envy aimed at confiscating wealth from others. In countries as varied as Taiwan, South Korea, Ghana, Mexico, Chile, and the former Soviet satellites in Eastern Europe, peaceful political reform has gone hand-in-hand with globalization.

Meanwhile, parts of the world that seethe the most with violence and domestic unrest—sub-Saharan Africa and the Middle East—are among the least open and democratic regions of the world, with each suffering declining shares of global trade and investment.

When Americans debate trade and globalization, more is at stake than promoting economic growth. Expanding trade and investment ties create a more peaceful and hospitable world, where hope for a brighter future can finally replace frustration and envy.

"Our [capitalist] economic system has competition at its heart, and that competition leads to war."

Capitalism Leads to War

Green Party of Great Britain

In the following viewpoint the Green Party of Great Britain argues that the untempered growth and competition inspired by capitalism leads to war. The capitalist spirit fuels the desire to succeed at any cost, encouraging companies to adopt risky economic policies such as excessive borrowing, the Green Party asserts. To prevent these companies from collapsing, the organization claims, capitalist nations declare war on "failed states" such as Iraq so that corporations can profit from the defense spending needed to go to war and gain access to the state's resources during rebuilding. Green Party candidates promote sustainable use of and equal access to stressed and dwindling resources.

As you read, consider the following questions:

1. In the opinion of the Green Party of Great Britain, what did Great Britain's taxpayers sacrifice to subsidize the arms industry?
2. What questions about the failure of Enron and other U.S. corporations were drowned out in the clamor over the need to defend the homeland after the September 11, 2001, terrorist attacks, in the author's view?
3. According to the author, what is true of almost all money in the modern economy?

Green Party of Great Britain, "War or Peace: A Stark Choice for the Direction of the Global Economy," *Green Party Budget Briefing*, 2004. Copyright © 2004 by the Green Party. Reproduced by permission.

W hatever happened to the peace dividend? A few years ago we heard much about the extra cash that would be available to spend on improving the quality of our lives now that the Cold War had ended. But there was merely the blink of an eye between the ending of that war and the finding of a new enemy and the creation of a new war. With Communism defeated Islam became the new enemy, and the war on terror was born.

This process was driven not by foreign policy objectives but by economic objectives. Our economic system has competition at its heart, and that competition leads to war. The engine of the global economy is profit, and the profits from the buying and selling of arms are huge. The [terrorist] threat to the US on September 11 [2001] was not primarily a threat to its citizens but a threat to its corporate heart: the symbolic target of the World Trade Center was chosen with care. The real cause of the war on terror was not [terrorist leader] Osama bin Laden and radical Islamicists but an economic system that is based in gross inequality and aggressive exploitation.

It is time that as citizens of one of the richest economies in the world [in Great Britain] we decide to spend that wealth to improve the quality of our lives, the lives of those in the poorest countries, and the lives of future generations. It is time we chose a peace economy rather than a war economy. . . .

The Real Costs of War

War is no longer a tool of foreign policy it is a major industry. The Green Deputy Mayor of London Jenny Jones revealed that she was shocked and horrified after her visit to this year's Defence Systems and Equipment International Exhibition at Docklands [England]:

> Over the years I've read reports of how the arms trade operates, but seeing at first hand this host of men from all over the world bargaining over weapons systems which bring death and misery to millions brings home how inhumane this industry is. This fair encourages the sale of weapons which kill hundreds of civilians just because they happen to be in the wrong place. I saw delegations from countries wracked with civil unrest, repression and poverty, and I couldn't help thinking of the millions of people in those

countries who don't have clean water or adequate food but do have expensively-equipped armies.

In the UK [United Kingdom] the arms industry is subsidised to the value of £420 million. This means that a substantial part of our taxes, that could be spent on hospitals, schools or sent as aid to the poorer countries of the world ends up in the pockets of arms industry executives.

Let's take the example of South Africa. In spite of its urgent development needs including an epidemic of AIDS and unemployment rates as high as 50 per cent in some of the black townships, in January 1999 Deputy Prime Minister Thabo Mbeki announced the cabinet's provisional approval of the decision to re-equip the South African National Defence Force (SANDF). The items to be procured include;

- 28 Gripen fighters from BAe/SAAB for £1.09 billion
- 24 Hawks trainer fighters from BAe for £470 million
- 4 corvettes-class patrol boats from a German shipbuilding consortium
- 3 diesel submarines from the German submarine consortium
- 4 super Lynx helicopters from GKN-Westland
- 40 light helicopters from the Italian firm Agusta in which GKN-Westland has a stake

The total programme is valued at £3 billion or R[Rand]29 billion. The costs, spread over fifteen years, will amount to an extra £200 million (or R2 billion) per annum, representing a 20% increase in the military budget. [British prime minister] Tony Blair has promised £4 billion worth of investments in South Africa in order to ensure that a sizeable proportion of the value of these purchases will go to UK companies. Export credit guarantees will be supplied to underwrite the risks inherent in the deal; in other words, we, as taxpayers, will be subsidising it.

The War on Terror Saved Capitalism

Remember Enron [a global energy and energy service provider]? When it went bust in November 2001 with debts of $20 billion backed by only $2 billion of assets it was the worst scandal capitalism had ever had to explain away. Fortunately for the executives of Enron, and other US corporations that had inflated their stock-market value with 'future value captured in the form of market capitalisation' as [accounting and consulting firm] Anderson call it in the fraudsters' training manual, such explanations were drowned out in the clamour over the need to defend the 'homeland' and the launching of the 'war on terror'. But this distraction was only one way in which this war prevented the collapse of several massive US corporations, and the potentially terminal destabilisation of the global economy this might cause.

Halliburton [a global energy service provider] with its $998 million debt, and the same taste in accounting advice, might have been next. It had used the same technique of 'unbilled receivables' to inflate the profits it reported to shareholders and the stock-market. The two companies shared many similarities: their place in the energy sector, vast borrowing, and close political ties with the White House. Like Enron they had postponed losses and counted money they had not even invoiced for as revenue, according to the pressure group Judicial Watch overstating profits to the value of $445 million during 1999 to 2001. Living on the accounting edge like this might have worked during the boom of the 1990s but was becoming impossible in the insecure new century, especially once the foundations of the corporate world were cracked by the World Trade Center attack and the fall of Enron.

Dick Cheney, chief executive of Halliburton from 1995 to 2000, and now Vice-President of the US was no doubt a keen supporter of the fantasticial 'war on terror' and the huge increase in defence spending it required. Halliburton almost immediately received billion-dollar contracts from the Pentagon to build operational bases. It was also saved from lawsuits it was facing from former employees who had been poisoned by asbestos, via a legal reform capping the value of such suits, causing Halliburton shares to rise by 43%. Cheney is not entirely in the clear: he is still facing a fraud case filed by Halliburton investors in the Dallas court [which as of this writing is still pending].

But Halliburton the company is now returned to the sorts of profits its shareholders enjoy. When [economist John] Keynes said that capitalism was about digging holes and fill-ing them in again he didn't have the [2003] war in Iraq in mind, but the aphorism fits. [President George W.] Bush's cronies have profited from the weapons that destroyed the country and are now gaining on the other side of the coin by winning multi-billion dollar contracts, paid for by Iraqi oil wealth, to repair the damage they caused against the will of the Iraqi people. War is certainly a profitable business.

A History of Profiting from War

During World War II, many of the wealthiest war profiteers, the very companies with controlling power in American society, joined in cartels with Nazi-run German industry, making agreements to limit the production and acquisition of vital war material (such as magnesium, tungsten carbide, and tetracene, for example). This and many other forms of cooperation between the American and German biggest industries before, during, and after the war, was exposed by socialists and other honest people during the war.

Profit-making was the engine that drove all the major countries, except the Soviet Union, in fighting World War II—not saving the Jews and other persecuted peoples of the world! Albanian Kosovars will be learning this bitter lesson under occupation, that the NATO [North Atlantic Treaty Organization] forces were not bombing them to save them, but to secure Yugoslavia—which, though moving towards capitalism, is still not a capitalist country—as a field for capitalist exploitation.

Carole Seligman, *Socialist Action*, October 1999.

Best of all, of course, you can declare a country a 'failed state' and take it over yourself. This allows you to set the prices of the tasty assets on display, and privilege your friends and family in the asset acquisition that follows. When the *Guardian* writer Julian Borger recently called his article 'Bush Cronies Advise on Buying Up Iraq', again he was not talking figuratively. Here is how his colleague Rory McCarthy in Baghdad, explained what is going on:

Under the new rules, announced by the finance minister, Kamil Mubdir al-Gailani, in Dubai, foreign firms will have the right to wholly own Iraqi companies, except those in the oil, gas and mineral industries. There will be no restrictions on the amount of profits that can be repatriated or on using local products. Corporate tax will be set at 15%.

And here again we see Halliburton, this time in the guise of its subsidiary Kellogg, Brown and Root, where Dick Cheney cut his corporate teeth, winning a big contract, this time worth $7 billion and again to repair Iraq's oil infrastructure. A company that was on the verge of a spectacular crash is now making good business again. Just one example of how the 'war on terror' has been a life-saver for US capitalism, with US growth figures moving from negative territory up to 4 per cent.

Thriving on Risk and Fear

The late phase of capitalism that we are living through prioritises risk. Risk-taking is now lauded and rewarded more than any other quality. Success stories under globalisation are based in borrowing money that you cannot possibly hope to pay back, and just hoping you will get away with it. The explanation for this extraordinary behaviour lies in the structure of our economic system and primarily the way money is created.

In the modern economy almost all money is created by being borrowed. So those who are prepared to borrow outrageous sums, unjustified by any assets they may have to back them up, are lauded and rewarded for their willingness to take risks. Without them the banks would not be able to bring money into existence and would not gain the face value of that money by doing so. Hence the sacred status of the entrepreneur. Because this money is lent with interest due, the entrepreneur must be able to find not only the lump sum, but also the additional value of the interest, hence his company must grow. Capitalism's obsession with growth is not an economic inevitability, only an inevitable consequence of a money system based on interest-bearing debt.

The other motivator for the enterpreneur is fear: fear of the risks he has taken, fear of failure, and above all fear of being a loser. Since our economy is typified by hierarchy nobody wants to end up anywhere else but on top of the dung-heap. Capitalism operates like a pump, where the energy of those who have least pushes them upwards to become those who have most; inequality is the motor that operates this pump. . . .

The Steady-State Economy

We need to step off the treadmill of growth and competition and build a steady-state economy. This means an end to economic growth and in many sectors it will mean a contraction of activity. A respect for planetary limits makes this inevitable. The addiction to economic growth is killing us all. In spite of the squeals from those who benefit from this economic system, surely your children's ability to breathe fresh air is worth more than a battery-powered cocktail stirrer? Do you really need a plasma TV if it means that the whole of the population of Kiribati will be displaced and thousands will drown in Bangladesh? These are the choices we are actually making every day. We should make the moral choice to cut our consumption and stop and smell the roses instead.

The competition for resources that is generating the wars and the injustice that gives rise to terrorism could also be ended by the move to the steady state. The economic energy that we have available without destroying the planet should be used to meet real human needs in the South as well as the West. Such a global compact based on fairness and justice would be an important step towards the peace that would give us more satisfaction than any number of consumer goods.

And finally, we need to build up strong local economies that would give us real security rather than leaving us at the mercy of corporations. The impulse towards increasing the quantity of goods produced locally and reducing the expansion of international trade came as a result of concern about the huge levels of carbon dioxide needlessly produced as biscuit-carrying juggernauts pass each other on Europe's congested road network, or as we find vegetables on our supermarket shelves grown in countries whose people are starving. As well as improving our quality of life and our human relationships a system of strong local economies would reinforce our identities as part of a functioning human community.

"Capitalism is the only political-economic system that protects individual rights by banning the initiation of force."

Capitalism Does Not Lead to War

Andrew Bernstein

In the following viewpoint Andrew Bernstein argues that capitalists do not use force but deal with others peacefully through free trade. Dictators who do not respect the rights of their own citizens are the ones who inspire war against other nations, he maintains. Capitalism, Bernstein asserts, protects individual economic and political freedom and bans the use of force, promoting prosperity and peace. Bernstein is a senior writer for the Ayn Rand Institute, a think tank devoted to promoting free trade and the rights of the individual.

As you read, consider the following questions:
1. What examples does Bernstein provide to support his opinion that the major wars of the twentieth century were started by dictatorial monarchies?
2. What examples does the author use to demonstrate that the Nobel Prize committee has repeatedly awarded its Peace Prize to the bringers of war?
3. According to the author, during what period did capitalism give mankind its longest period of peace?

Andrew Bernstein, "Of War and Peace; Does the Nobel Panel Understand the Cause of War?" *Washington Times*, October 16, 2002, p. A19. Copyright © 2002 by News World Communications, Inc. Reproduced by permission.

The Nobel Peace Prize was just awarded to Jimmy Carter [in 2002]. Although Mr. Carter's efforts to convince Egypt to recognize Israel's right to exist was a genuine achievement, he has otherwise continuously betrayed the principles on which peace depend.

For many years Mr. Carter, espousing collectivist ideals, has traipsed the globe treating aggressor and victim with equal respect. For example, he aided the nuclear program of North Korea, the most repressive dictatorship on Earth and part of the axis of evil. Mr. Carter's trip [in May 2002] to Cuba, where he sanctioned and supported the dictator Fidel Castro, is just more . . . evidence that he understands nothing of rights and peace. In choosing Mr. Carter, the Nobel Committee has shown yet again that it does not understand the cause of war and so of peace.

Dictatorial Regimes Cause Wars

To understand the cause of war, consider the major wars of the 20th century. World War I was started by the dictatorial monarchies of Germany and Russia. Nazi Germany caused World War II by invading Poland. Totalitarian Soviet Russia repeatedly initiated war by first aligning with Hitler in the conquest of Poland, then by swallowing up Eastern Europe in 1945, and later by supporting the communist invasion of South Korea.

And consider . . . less global conflicts. [Iraqi leader] Saddam Hussein instigated the Persian Gulf War by conquering Kuwait. The Taliban, former dictators of Afghanistan, warred against other factions in Afghanistan and then spread its terror overseas by arming and abetting Osama bin Laden's [terrorist] attacks against the United States [on September 11, 2001].

Observe the pattern. It is the less-free nations—those in which power is concentrated in the hands of the state at the expense of the individual—that attack their freer neighbors. Such statist regimes are the cause of history's most savage wars. Statist regimes launched the wars that ravaged much of the world in the 20th century. The reason why these regimes did so is not difficult to find.

Dictators are in chronic war against their own people.

Hitler murdered the Jews. Stalin, Mao and Pol Pot [of Cambodia] each murdered millions of businessmen, landowners and bourgeoisie. [Serbian president] Slobodan Milosevic slaughtered the Muslims. Saddam butchered the Kurds. In her seminal essay, "The Roots of War," Ayn Rand observed: "A country that violates the rights of its own citizens, will not respect the rights of its neighbors. Those who do not recognize individuals' rights, will not recognize the rights of nations: a nation is only a number of individuals."

Destructive Acts Do Not Lead to Prosperity

Capitalism neither requires nor promotes imperialist expansion. Capitalism did not create imperialism or warfare. Warlike societies predate societies with secure private property. The idea that inequity or underspending give rise to militarism lacks any rational basis. Imperialistic tendencies exist due to ethnic and nationalistic bigotries, and the want for power. Prosperity depends upon our ability to *prevent* destructive acts. The dogma of destructive creation fails as a silver lining to the cloud of warfare. Destructive acts entail real costs that diminish available opportunities.

D.W. MacKenzie, Ludwig von Mises Institute, www.mises.org, April 10, 2003.

Statism is the cause of war.

Statism rests on the idea that men can legitimately pursue their ends by initiating force against other men. In a free country, such acts are properly regarded as criminal and punished by law. In a free country, government uses force only in retaliation against those who initiate it.

But statist regimes of all varieties—Nazi, communist, Islamic fundamentalist, etc.—initiate force ceaselessly against innocent victims, first within their own borders and then without. In a free country, it is recognized that every individual has an inalienable right to his own life. In a statist country, the individual exists in bondage to the state, his life to be sacrificed at the whim of the state.

Rewarding the Bringers of War

Shamefully, the Nobel committee has repeatedly awarded its Peace Prize to the bringers of war.

For example, it routinely bestows the prize on statists who

condemn the United States—the world's freest, most individualistic country—while praising murderous Third World dictatorships. It awarded the 1994 prize to Yasser Arafat, the [former] brutal dictator of the Palestinian Authority, who imposed a despotic regime on his own people and initiated a murderous war against the free citizens of Israel. Even worse, in 1973 it awarded the prize to Le Duc Tho, the North Vietnamese communist, who, along with Ho Chi Minh and other party leaders, imposed a vicious communist dictatorship in North Vietnam that slaughtered at least 50,000 Vietnamese in the 1950s, and then invaded and conquered South Vietnam. All told, the death toll caused by that communist dictatorship and its warring totaled 2 million individuals.

If one admires men who cause war, one will ignore or vilify men who promote peace. Those who respect and support individual rights and political-economic freedom are the only true lovers of peace. Private capitalists and businessmen are outstanding examples. Business requires the barring of the initiation of force. Businessmen deal with one another peacefully, by means of trade, persuasion and voluntary contracts and agreements. Because businessmen respect the rights of all individuals, they have helped liberate the best minds to innovate, invent and advance, and thereby helped produce great general prosperity and peace. By helping to spread free trade across the globe, they have created peaceful relations among the individuals of many nations. Yet, perversely, capitalists are denounced as exploiters of man.

Values That Promote Peace

If we sincerely seek to attain the inestimable value that is world peace, it is individual rights and, therefore, capitalism that we must endorse. Capitalism is the only political-economic system that protects individual rights by banning the initiation of force. As Ayn Rand observed, it was capitalism that gave mankind its longest period of peace—an era in which there were no wars involving the entire civilized world—from the end of the Napoleonic Wars in 1815 to the outbreak of World War I in 1914.

If we truly want to recognize and promote the cause of peace, let us award a peace prize to capitalism.

"[Peaceniks] are acting to make war more frequent and deadly, by making our enemies more aggressive, more plentiful, and more powerful."

Pacifism Escalates War

Alex Epstein

By asking governments to ignore acts of aggression, pacifists inspire war, argues Alex Epstein in the following viewpoint. Pacifist-inspired inaction, he claims, sends the message to aggressors that they can attack without being subjected to retaliation. According to Epstein, history illustrates that the only way to deal with aggression is to fight back, showing enemies that if they attack, they will be destroyed. Epstein writes for the Ayn Rand Institute, a think tank devoted to promoting free trade and the rights of the individual.

As you read, consider the following questions:
1. In Epstein's opinion, why is pacifism an inherently negative doctrine?
2. What will happen if the United States fails to use its military against state sponsors of terrorism, in the author's view?
3. According to Epstein, from where does the suicidal stance of peaceniks come?

There is an increasingly vocal movement that seeks to engage America in ever longer, wider, and more costly wars—leading to thousands and perhaps millions of unnecessary deaths. This movement calls itself the "anti-war" movement.

Across America and throughout the world, "anti-war" groups are staging "peace rallies" that attract tens, sometimes hundreds of thousands of participants who gather to voice their opposition to an invasion of Iraq and to any other U.S. military action in the war on terrorism.

The goal of these rallies, the protesters proclaim, is to promote peace. "You can bomb the world to pieces," they chant, "but you can't bomb it into peace."

Platitudes Without Answers

If dropping bombs won't work, what *should* the United States do to obtain a peaceful relationship with the numerous hostile regimes, including Iraq, that seek to harm us with terrorism and weapons of mass destruction? "Peace advocates" offer no answer. The most one can coax out of them are vague platitudes (we should "make common cause with the people of the world," says the prominent "anti-war" group Not in Our Name) and agonized soul-searching ("Why do they hate us?").

The absence of a peacenik peace plan is no accident. Pacifism is inherently a negative doctrine—it merely says that military action is always bad. As one San Francisco protester put the point: "I don't think it's right for our government to kill people." In practice, this leaves the government only two means of dealing with our enemies: to *ignore* their acts of aggression, or to *appease* them by capitulating to the aggressor's demands.

The Consequences of Pacifism

We do not need to predict or deduce the consequences of pacifism with regard to terrorism and the nations that sponsor it, because we *experienced* those consequences [when terrorists attacked] on September 11 [2001].

Pacifism practically dictated the American response to terrorism for more than 23 years, beginning with our government's response to the first major act of Islamic terrorism against this country when Iranian mobs held 52 Americans hostage for 444 days at the American embassy in Tehran.

Pacifists Have Blood on Their Hands

Pacifists of the 20th century had a lot of blood on their hands for weakening the Western democracies in the face of rising belligerence and military might in aggressor nations like Nazi Germany and imperial Japan. In Britain during the 1930s, Labor Party members of Parliament voted repeatedly against military spending, while Hitler built up the most powerful military machine in Europe. Students at leading British universities signed pledges to refuse to fight in the event of war.

All of this encouraged the Nazis and the Japanese toward war against countries that they knew had greater military potential than their own. Military potential only counts when there is the will to develop it and use it, and the fortitude to continue with a bloody war when it comes. This is what they did not believe the West had. And it was Western pacifists who led them to that belief.

Thomas Sowell, Townhall.com, September 24, 2001.

In response to that and later terrorist atrocities, American presidents sought to avoid military action at all costs, treating terrorists as isolated criminals and thereby ignoring the role of the governments that support them, or by offering diplomatic handouts to terrorist states in hopes that they would want to be our friends. With each pacifist response it became clearer that the most powerful nation on Earth was a paper tiger—and our enemies made the most of it.

After years of American politicians acting like peaceniks, Islamic terrorism has proliferated from a few gangs of thugs to a worldwide scourge—making possible the attacks of September 11.

Inviting Acts of War

It is an obvious evasion of history and logic for advocates of pacifism to label themselves "anti-war," since the policies they advocate necessarily invite escalating acts of war against anyone who practices them. Military inaction sends the mes-

sage to an aggressor—and to other, potential aggressors—
that it will benefit by attacking the United States. To whatever extent "anti-war" protesters influence policy, they are
not helping to prevent war; they are acting to make war
more frequent and deadly, by making our enemies more aggressive, more plentiful, and more powerful.

Force Is the Best Solution

The only way to deal with militant enemies is to show them
unequivocally that aggression against the United States will
lead to their destruction. The only means of imparting this
lesson is overwhelming military force—enough to defeat and
incapacitate the enemy.

Had we annihilated the Iranian regime 23 years ago, we
could have thwarted Islamic terrorism at the beginning, with
far less cost than will be required to defeat terrorism today.

And if we fail to use our military against state sponsors of
terrorism today, imagine the challenge we will face five years
from now when Iraq and Iran possess nuclear weapons and
are ready to disseminate them to their terrorist minions. Yet
such a world is the goal of the "anti-war" movement.

The suicidal stance of peaceniks is no innocent error or
mere overflow of youthful idealism. It is the product of a fundamentally immoral commitment: the commitment to ignore
reality—from the historical evidence of the consequences of
pacifism to the very existence of the violent threats that confront us today—in favor of the wish that laying down our arms
will achieve peace *somehow*.

Those of us who are committed to facing the facts should
condemn these peaceniks for what they really are: warmon-
gers for our enemies.

> *"Wars produce war-like societies, which, in turn, make the world more dangerous for other societies."*

Warlike Societies Perpetuate War

Barbara Ehrenreich

According to Barbara Ehrenreich, wars create warlike societies that prompt other societies to become prone to war in self-defense. War is like a parasite, Ehrenreich claims; she asserts, for example, that the costs of war and self-defense are so high that a nation's military can deplete the country's resources at the detriment of its own people. War is also like an epidemic disease, she argues, because it insidiously spreads from one war-prone society to the next. Ehrenreich, a *Progressive* columnist, is author of *Blood Rites: Origins and History of the Passions of War.*

As you read, consider the following questions:

1. According to Ehrenreich, what is it tempting to conclude from the fact that warfare is so ubiquitous and historically commonplace among humans?
2. In the author's opinion, what is contrary to the biological theories of war?
3. Why was Karl Marx wrong about what shapes societies, in the author's view?

Only three types of creatures engage in warfare—humans, chimpanzees, and ants. Among humans, warfare is so ubiquitous and historically commonplace that we are often tempted to attribute it to some innate predisposition for slaughter—a gene, perhaps, manifested as a murderous hormone. The earliest archeological evidence of war is from 12,000 years ago, well before such innovations as capitalism and cities and at the very beginning of settled, agricultural life. Sweeping through recorded history, you can find a predilection for warfare among hunter-gatherers, herding and farming peoples, industrial and even post-industrial societies, democracies, and dictatorships. The good old pop-feminist explanation—testosterone—would seem, at first sight, to fit the facts.

War Is Not an Instinct

But war is too complex and collective an activity to be accounted for by any war-like instinct lurking within the individual psyche. Battles, in which the violence occurs, are only one part of war, most of which consists of preparation for battle—training, the manufacture of weapons, the organization of supply lines, etc. There is no plausible instinct, for example, that could impel a man to leave home, cut his hair short, and drill for hours in tight formation.

Contrary to the biological theories of war, it is not easy to get men to fight. In recent centuries, men have often gone to great lengths to avoid war—fleeing their homelands, shooting off their index fingers, feigning insanity. So unreliable was the rank and file of the famed eighteenth century Prussian army that military rules forbade camping near wooded areas: The troops would simply melt away into the trees. Even when men are duly assembled for battle, killing is not something that seems to come naturally to them. As Lieutenant Colonel Dave Grossman argued in his book *On Killing: The Psychological Cost of Learning to Kill in War and Society*, one of the great challenges of military training is to get soldiers to shoot directly at individual enemies.

War Reproduces Itself

What is it, then, that has made war such an inescapable part of the human experience? Each war, of course, appears to

CANNIBAL

the participants to have an immediate purpose—to crush the "Hun," preserve democracy, disarm [Iraqi leader Saddam Hussein], or whatever—that makes it noble and necessary. But those who study war dispassionately, as a recurrent event with no moral content, have observed a certain mathematical pattern: that of "epidemicity," or the tendency of war to spread in the manner of an infectious disease. Obviously, war is not a symptom of disease or the work of microbes, but it does spread geographically in a disease-like manner, usually as groups take up warfare in response to war-like neighbors. It also spreads through time, as the losses suffered in one war call forth new wars of retaliation. Think of World War I, which breaks out for no good reason at all, draws in most of

Europe as well as the United States, and then "reproduces" itself, after a couple of decades, as World War II.

In other words, as the Dutch social scientist Henk Houweling puts it, "one of the causes of war is war itself." Wars produce war-like societies, which, in turn, make the world more dangerous for other societies, which are thus recruited into being war-prone themselves. Just as there is no gene for war, neither is there a single type or feature of society—patriarchy or hierarchy—that generates it. War begets war and shapes human societies as it does so.

In general, war shapes human societies by requiring that they possess two things: one, some group or class of men (and, in some historical settings, women) who are trained to fight; and, two, the resources to arm and feed them. These requirements have often been compatible with patriarchal cultures dominated by a warrior elite—knights or samurai—as in medieval Europe or Japan. But not always: Different ways of fighting seem to lead to different forms of social and political organization. Historian Victor Hansen has argued that the phalanx formation adopted by the ancient Greeks, with its stress on equality and interdependence, was a factor favoring the emergence of democracy among non-slave Greek males. And there is no question but that the mass, gun-wielding armies that appeared in Europe in the seventeenth century contributed to the development of the modern nation-state—if only as a bureaucratic apparatus to collect the taxes required to support those armies.

Marx was wrong, then: It is not only the "means of production" that shape societies, but the means of destruction. In our own time, the costs of war, or war-readiness, are probably larger than at any time in history, in relation to other human needs, due to the pressure on nations not only to maintain a mass standing army—the United States supports about a million men and women at arms—but to keep up with an extremely expensive, ever-changing technology of killing. The cost squeeze has led to a new type of society perhaps best termed a "depleted" state, in which the military has drained resources from all other social functions. North Korea is a particularly ghoulish example, where starvation coexists with nuclear weapons development. But the USSR also crumbled under the weight of militarism, and the United States brandishes its military might around the world while, at this moment, cutting school lunches and health care for the poor.

"Addiction" provides only a pallid and imprecise analogy for the human relationship to war; parasitism—or even predation—is more to the point. However and whenever war began, it has persisted and propagated itself with the terrifying tenacity of a beast attached to the neck of living prey, feeding on human effort and blood.

If this is what we are up against, it won't do much good to try to uproot whatever war-like inclinations may dwell within our minds. Abjuring violent speech and imagery, critiquing masculinist culture, and promoting respect for human diversity—all of those are worthy projects, but they will make little contribution to the abolition of war. It would be far better to think of war as something external to ourselves, something which has to be uprooted, everywhere, down to the last weapon and bellicose pageant.

The "epidemicity" of war has one other clear implication: War cannot be used as a means to prevent or abolish war. True, for some time to come, urgent threats from other heavily armed states will require at least the threat of armed force in response. But these must be very urgent threats and extremely restrained responses. To indulge, one more time, in the metaphor of war as a kind of living thing, a parasite on human societies: The idea of a war to end war is one of its oldest, and cruelest, tricks.

Periodical Bibliography

The following articles have been selected to supplement the diverse views presented in this chapter.

Ed Ayres	"It's Not About Oil!" *World Watch*, May/June 2003.
Kurt M. Campbell	"Globalization's First War?" *Washington Quarterly*, Winter 2002.
Chris Edwards	"The UN Has Predicted Several Times That There Would Be Wars over Water. Have Any Happened?" *Geographical*, November 2003.
Joseph Gerson	"Roots of War, Roots of Resistance," *Z Magazine*, January 31, 2002.
John Gray	"Staving Off Disaster: The Interaction of Weak States and Deadly New Weapons Could Give Birth to a Tragic Century," *Guardian*, September 28, 2001.
David Gushee	"Holy War: When Religion Goes Sour," *Baptist Standard*, November 5, 2001.
Thomas Hayden	"The Roots of War: Can Humanity Ever Escape Its Age-Old Legacy of Battle?" *U.S. News & World Report*, April 26, 2004.
Mark Lattimer	"Measuring Civilization," *UN Chronicle*, 2002.
Richard Ned Lebow	"Contingency, Catalysts, and International System Change," *Political Science Quarterly*, Winter 2000.
Thomas Merton	"The Root of War Is Fear," *National Catholic Reporter*, April 4, 2003.
Pugwash Conferences on Science and World Affairs	"Eliminating the Causes of War," *Pugwash Online: Conferences on Science and World Affairs*, August 2000. Available at www.pugwash.org.
Peter Ryan	"Humanity's Crimes," *Quadrant*, March 1999.
Mark Townsend	"Water Fight Is Looming; Water—or the Lack of It—Threatens to Become One of the Single Biggest Factors Opposing World Peace," *Geographical*, April 2002.

CHAPTER 2

When Is War Justified?

Chapter Preface

Many citizens of the United States believe that the March 2003 invasion of Iraq to oust Iraqi leader Saddam Hussein was not justified. Nevertheless, the Bush administration, claiming that the president has the authority to make such a decision, decided to proceed with the invasion. Some authorities argue, however, that the decision whether or not a U.S. war is justified should not be made by the president but instead by the people, through their representatives in Congress. Who should decide when the United States is justified in going to war has been the subject of debate since the nation's founding.

One complaint that American colonists leveled against King George III of England in the 1776 Declaration of Independence was that he, not the citizens, held the power to make war. The colonists objected to being forced to help pay the price of King George's war against France. Nearly a century later Abraham Lincoln acknowledged the threat posed by war powers placed solely in the hands of rulers in an 1848 letter:

> Kings had always been involving and impoverishing their people in wars, pretending generally, if not always, that the good of the people was the object. This, our [Constitutional] Convention understood to be the most oppressive of all Kingly oppressions; and they resolved to so frame the Constitution that no one man should hold the power of bringing this oppression upon us.

Indeed, the Founding Fathers wrote the Constitution in such a way that the power to wage war was divided between the legislative and executive branches. The Constitution gives Congress the power to declare war, raise and support armies, and provide and maintain a navy, making the president commander in chief of the army and navy. The document gives Congress control of the money to finance the military and the president the job of leading it. However, despite the founders' intentions, strong presidents have been able to get around this division of authority. Journalist Sean McCollum asserts, "The right 'to declare war' is where history and practice have muddied the rules. Although Congress specifically holds the power to declare war, it has been the president who has sent soldiers, sailors, and pilots into combat."

Despite efforts by Congress to limit the president's power to send troops to war, American presidents continue to do so in undeclared wars such as Korea, Grenada, Somalia, Kosovo, Afghanistan, and Iraq. As American casualties mounted in the Vietnam War, a war never officially approved by Congress, public outrage rose, particularly when Americans learned that their government had misled them about the war's justification and its progress. Americans were told repeatedly that the military was making headway. In fact, the enemy proved to be resilient, and American soldiers continued to die. Thus, in 1973 Congress responded with the War Powers Resolution to "insure that the collective judgment of both Congress and the President will apply to the introduction of the United States Armed Forces into hostilities." The law increased communication between the president and Congress, and no president since its enactment has sent troops into combat without some form of congressional involvement. However, claims law professor Michael C. Dorf,

> Critics who believe that Congress should have more effective checks on Presidential war making powers have observed that the War Powers Resolution does little to accomplish this goal. . . . [T]he formal need for Congressional approval is superseded by the political impossibility of Congress's withholding that approval once the President has unilaterally committed troops.

Those who support presidential war-making power argue that it is necessary for defensive purposes. The president, they argue, must be given the ability to respond instantly to foreign crises to protect American lives or prevent irreparable damage to U.S. interests. In such cases, involving Congress, which they claim moves too slowly, is impractical. Critics of these arguments such as attorney Doug Bandow answer that few presidential wars have been defensive. "There was nothing defensive about overthrowing ruling regimes in Panama and Haiti. . . . Nor was there anything defensive about joining the conflict between Kuwait and Iraq," he claims.

Analysts in the United States continue to debate whether Congress or the president should decide whether going to war is justified. The authors in the following chapter discuss other points of controversy in debates about when war is justified.

> "*Some threats to peace, to freedom, and to the minimum conditions of world order can only be met by hard [military] power.*"

War Is Sometimes Justified to Maintain Peace and Promote Freedom

George Weigel

The United States has the moral duty to go to war to maintain peace and promote freedom, argues George Weigel in the following viewpoint. When nations exhaust efforts to uphold international law through diplomatic efforts ("soft power"), contends Weigel, military action ("hard power") is justified. Mature policy makers do not appease those who threaten peace and freedom, claims Weigel, but use military power to demonstrate that international lawbreakers will be punished. Weigel is a senior fellow at the Ethics and Public Policy Center.

As you read, consider the following questions:
1. What was President George W. Bush's response to Cardinal Pio Laghi's claim that there must be another way to disarm Iraq than military force?
2. In Weigel's view, what has Jonathan Schell failed to take into account in his book *The Unconquerable World?*
3. With what does Weigel believe the just-war tradition begins?

George Weigel, "The Morality of War," *Commentary*, vol. 116, July/August 2003, p. 50. Copyright © 2003 by the American Jewish Committee. Reproduced by permission of the publisher and the author.

A mid the welter of moral argument—some serious, much not—that preceded Operation Iraqi Freedom [the March 2003 invasion of Iraq], two clarifying moments stand out.

The first came on January 26 [2003], when Secretary of State Colin Powell addressed a generally hostile audience of the global great and good in Davos, Switzerland. After having made the case for a possible armed intervention in Iraq, Powell was asked by George Carey, the . . . retired Archbishop of Canterbury, whether the Bush administration was not overselling the capacity of "hard power" to change what needed changing in the world, and underrating the utility of "soft power." The terms are the trope of the Harvard political scientist Joseph Nye; soft power, in Carey's less than luminous formulation, has "something to do with human values."

The Uses of Hard and Soft Power

Powell, an Episcopalian and long the most reluctant of the administration's senior officials to use hard power in Iraq, had had enough. "There is nothing in American experience or in American political life or in our culture that suggests that we want to use hard power," he replied, and went on:

> But what we have found over the decades is that unless you do have hard power—and here I think you're referring to military power—then sometimes you are faced with situations that you can't deal with. . . . It was not soft power that freed Europe [in the 1940's]. It was hard power. And what followed immediately after hard power? Did the United States ask for dominion over a single nation in Europe? No. Soft power came in with the Marshall Plan [to reconstruct Europe]. Soft power came with American GI's who put their weapons down once the war was over and helped those nations rebuild. We did the same thing in Japan.

Five and a half weeks later, on March 5, Cardinal Pio Laghi—former Vatican ambassador in Washington, personal friend of former President George H.W. Bush, and now Pope John Paul II's special envoy—met in the Oval Office with President George W. Bush. The President reviewed the administration's case against [Iraqi leader] Saddam Hussein and the reasons leading inexorably to the conclusion that Iraq could be disarmed only by the use of military force. In response, Cardinal Laghi urged that there must be "another way." To which the President replied, crisply, that all the "other ways" had been tried and had not worked; anyone serious about the disarmament of Iraq had to recognize that.

Strip away the barnacles attached to the massive peace demonstrations that roiled the West's major cities in February and March [2003]—anti-globalization, anti-Israel, anti-"racism," anti-McDonald's, anti-America, anti-whatever—and you will find the same conviction: there had to be another way than military force. . . .

But something else was also afoot in the pre-war debate, particularly among those who came to the argument equipped with strong moral convictions. That something was the resolute refusal to acknowledge that, in the world as it is and as it will remain, soft power must be buttressed by hard power in the pursuit of peace.

The Advocates of Soft Power

The refusal itself is not a new phenomenon; once upon a time, and not so long ago at that, it could be attributed to political naïveté, to a misreading of the Sermon on the Mount, to utopianism, or to some combination thereof. Today, however, it bears a new face, and has marshaled new evidence to advance its claims. Appealing to the manifest accomplishments of the late-20th-century human-rights movement, advocates of soft power adduce such successes as the largely nonviolent revolution of 1989 in Eastern and Central Europe; the Filipino "people power" revolution of 1985–86; and the democratic transformations in East Asia and Latin America. What these examples suggest is that, in some circumstances, there may indeed be another way. What a fair number of people have concluded from them is that, especially where the exercise of American power looms as the alternative, there must always be another way. . . .

Examining the Soft-Power Approach

Perhaps the most ambitious effort, [after the September 11, 2001, terrorist attacks] to argue for the necessity of a comprehensive soft-power approach to international conflict is Jonathan Schell's *The Unconquerable World: Power, Nonviolence, and the Will of the People*. . . .

The Unconquerable World does get some things right. Europe's settling down to four years of internecine slaughter in August 1914 was indeed one of history's great divides. By contrast, the nonviolent revolution of 1989 was a powerful demonstration that "the moral equivalent of war" (to use [psychologist and philosopher] William James's phrase) could change things for the better. Just as Schell writes, moreover, consent is the essence of political stability, and when consent is withdrawn, even the most solid-seeming regimes can crumble. The human-rights movement is indeed a powerful factor in contemporary world politics, and its successes do demonstrate that hard power is not the only form of power. Finally, the expanding world of the democracies is an expanding world of peace, one in which the problem of war has been largely solved. . . .

As Schell notes, "cooperative" power has expanded its sway in the world over the past century, and the democratic world, which embodies such cooperative power within and among states, constitutes a remarkable zone of peace. Yet there is no reckoning in *The Unconquerable World* with the present dangers to this zone of peace. Islamism is a minor blip on Schell's threat-acquisition radar, and China's potential for mischief of various sorts goes simply unremarked. . . .

A Vulnerable World

Schell is also tone-deaf to the crucial role of culture in contemporary international politics. Over the last 400 years, he suggests, the "war system" has been Europe's principal contribution to history, thus ignoring law, science, and the arts. The "logic" of this "war system," he writes, means that wars always "run to extremes," thus ignoring such contrary evidence as America's 20th-century military interventions in Central America and the Caribbean, the Korean war, or, more recently, the Six-Day war, the first Gulf war, and Afghanistan [in 2001]. Imperialism, he sums up, is nothing but "a mature, well-developed structure of violence," ignoring the fact that the British empire, for all its faults, brought the soft power of the rule of law to places where it had never been before (South Asia) and has not been since (the Middle East, with the exception of Israel). And so forth.

Finally, in this lengthy book on contemporary problems of international security, there is no mention of the Khobar Towers bombing, the terrorist attacks on U.S. embassies in East Africa, and al Qaeda's attack on the U.S.S. *Cole*. Others may remember, however, that each of these incidents took place on the watch of an American administration deeply committed to soft power [Bill Clinton's administration]. What this suggests is that a world in which the accomplishments of soft power are not protected by the availability of hard power, and by the willingness to use it in defense of those accomplishments, is not an "unconquerable" world at all. It is a profoundly vulnerable world.

A Need for Hard Power

Indeed, some threats to peace, to freedom, and to the minimum conditions of world order can only be met by hard power. Moreover, while cooperative power is certainly a civilizational accomplishment of the first importance, there are instances in which it cannot be deployed because the adversary will read it as weakness and intensify his aggression. If Israel had chosen "another way" in 1948, the Jews would have been driven into the sea in a mass slaughter. On the other hand, if the Palestinian Arabs had chosen "another way" after the Six-Day war of 1967, they would now be making preparations to celebrate the 35th anniversary of their state. But complexities like these are not to be imagined in the world according to Jonathan Schell.

Where they are indeed imagined, and deeply pondered, is in the body of thought known as the just-war tradition. Contrary to many contemporary confusions—frequently propagated, alas, by churchmen—the just-war tradition is not simply a method of casuistry: a series of hurdles, primarily having to do with the protection of non-combatants, that religious leaders and moral philosophers set for public officials. Rather, it is a theory of statecraft, a method for determining when and how hard power can contribute to securing the political goods of freedom, justice, and peace (understood as order). The just-war tradition, in other words, is about linking good ends to the means capable of achieving those ends. For to will good ends without willing the means to them is frivolity, a form of moral childishness.

In her new book, *Just War Against Terror: The Burden of American Power in a Violent World*, Jean Bethke Elshtain lays out the case for moral adulthood in contemporary international politics. She opens her book with a chilling injunction from Osama bin Laden, in which the al Qaeda chieftain calls on "every Muslim who believes in Allah and wishes to be rewarded to comply with Allah's order to kill the Americans and plunder their money wherever and whenever they find it."

A Moral Duty

Anyone, Elshtain suggests, who refuses to reckon with the reality of this bloody-minded charge, or with the threat it poses to the accomplishments of soft power in the United States and throughout the West, belongs in the company of the humane fools in [Albert] Camus's novel, *The Plague*, who refuse to believe that there are rats in the city and thereby make the plague worse. Since today's plague-bearers are all too real, we "have no choice but to fight—not in order to conquer any countries or to destroy peoples or religions, but to defend who we are and what we, at our best, represent." In the circumstances faced by the United States, the use of hard power is not simply one option among many; it is a moral duty.

A Time for War

There are times when the world can not sit by and watch evil roam unfettered. When people are being systematically massacred by murderous leaders, war is necessary. When the cause is just and the threat is real, war is necessary. Unfortunately in our age of global terrorism wrought by Islamic fundamentalists, war is necessary. In these tragic scenarios and several others, war is necessary.

James Weinstein, *Mantic Eye*, September 19, 2002.

Just War Against Terror takes a classically Augustinian approach [that is, following the doctrine of St. Augustine] to the body of thought out of which it grows. Governments, Elshtain writes, exist to ensure "civic peace." This civic peace is "not the kingdom promised by Scripture that awaits the end-time" but, rather, a humbler thing: a "basic framework of settled law and simple, everyday order." This—the very conditions for the possibility of civil peace—is what terrorists and rogue states seek to destroy or disrupt, and that is why the first moral duty of governments in the face of such a threat is to stop it. Although it seems an elementary point, it is one that the advocates of soft power seem to have had no end of trouble grasping.

The Ends of War

The next step in the just-war tradition is to recognize the moral distinctiveness of war. As Elshtain notes, principled pacifists, functional pacifists (like Jonathan Schell), and hardened realists all agree that war exists in a realm beyond moral reasoning and argument. But the just-war tradition takes a different tack, rigorously distinguishing between, on the one hand, the violence of brigandage, piracy, or modern terrorism and, on the other hand, the proportionate and discriminate use of armed force by legitimate public authorities for morally defensible ends. In other words, war is a moral category, and peace, in Elshtain's formulation, "may sometimes be served by the just use of force, even as power is most certainly involved."

The just-war tradition does not, then, begin with a "presumption against war" or a "presumption against violence," as so many religious leaders and intellectuals since 9/11 and particularly during the debate before Operation Iraqi Freedom have claimed. Rather, it begins with the question of ends. Only after having established the ends that public authority is obliged to seek and to defend does it take up the question of means.

This latter question is of course never easy—especially when it comes to an asymmetrical conflict like the one between a state (the United States) and terrorist organizations that function like states but do not have the "location" of a state in the international system (al Qaeda, Hizballah, Hamas). Still, Elshtain observes, morally serious adults "have to discern where self-defense begins and ends, where just punishment begins and ends, how to distinguish each of these from revenge and vengeance, how to build in limits against foes who preach and practice violence and killing without limits, and so on." By recognizing that war is a human activity that, like every other human activity, falls within the scrutiny of moral reason, the just-war tradition offers a very different picture of our situation from the one on offer in Jonathan Schell's image of a "war system" with an innate and irresistible tendency toward "extremes."

In the event, Operation Iraqi Freedom would pose a test of these two ideas, and would convincingly demonstrate which is the more accurate. As we saw in that conflict, contemporary weapons technologies make it far less likely that war waged by a responsible combatant like the United States will inevitably escalate into mass slaughter, and far more likely that it will take account of the principles of proportionality (no more force than necessary) and discrimination (no direct targeting of noncombatants) demanded by the just-war tradition. Global satellite positioning systems, precision-guided munitions, and stealth technologies are all costly. But far from being indicators of American imperial ambitions or strategic recklessness, let alone Schell's "logic" of "extremes," the use of these remarkable weapons, which in Iraq destroyed a totalitarian regime without destroying the country it had held in thrall, indicates American moral and political seriousness. . . .

Sanctioning Force Against Lawbreakers

Legal, political, and diplomatic means of resolving conflict, morally and politically desirable as they may be, are not always adaptable to threats that cannot be ignored: German and Japanese ambitions in the 1930's, genocidal ethnic cleansing in the Balkans, an Iraqi regime bent on developing nuclear weapons. A millennium and a half of Western reflection suggests, furthermore, that armed force can and does contribute to the rule of law in international affairs by demonstrating that lawbreakers will pay for their aggression and will not be permitted to destroy the minimum conditions of order in politics among nations.

How could it be otherwise? Imagine a world that had "evolved" to the point where there really were effective legal and political institutions and instruments for resolving conflicts among nations. Even in that world, the rule of law would not be self-vindicating. Human nature being what it is, someone would inevitably break the rules, and would do so at times and in ways that could not be handled by diplomacy. Even in such a world, then, the sanction of proportionate and discriminate armed force would have to remain available, precisely to vindicate the rule of law. "Hard power" and "soft power" are two dimensions of the morally serious exercise of power.

The war that began on 9/11 is, in many respects, a war against deeply entrenched fantasies. The notion that soft power and hard power are antinomies is one such fantasy, on a par with the claim that the Security Council as presently constituted is an inherently superior moral authority. What Americans learned on 9/11 is that the world is too dangerous to allow these fantasies further sway. It is past time for all those who wish to think about world politics in moral categories to learn that same lesson.

> *"Acts of violence committed in 'justice' or in affirmation of 'rights' or in defense of 'peace' do not end violence."*

War Does Not Maintain Peace or Promote Freedom

Wendell Berry

Justifying war in the name of freedom and peace is absurd and hypocritical, claims Wendell Berry in the following viewpoint. Claims that sanctioned violence will prevent unsanctioned violence are ridiculous, he argues, and going to war against another nation for manufacturing weapons that the United States itself produces is hypocritical. War only leads to move violence and inequity in the world, Berry concludes. Berry, a poet, philosopher, and conservationist, farms in Kentucky.

As you read, consider the following questions:

1. In Berry's view, what has modern war made it impossible to do?
2. According to the author, why is hypocrisy about violence inescapable in the current century?
3. How is the accounting of the price of war similar to our accounting of "the price of progress," in Berry's opinion?

Wendell Berry, "The Failure of War," *YES! Magazine*, Winter 2001–2002 and *Citizenship Papers*. New York: Shoemaker & Hoard, 2003. Copyright © 2003 by Wendell Berry. Reproduced by permission of Shoemaker & Hoard and *YES! Magazine*, PO Box 10818, Bainbridge Island, WA 98001. Subscriptions: 800-937-4451. Web: www.yesmagazine.org.

If you know even as little history as I do, it is hard not to doubt the efficacy of modern war as a solution to any problem except that of retribution—the "justice" of exchanging one damage for another.

Apologists for war will insist that war answers the problem of national self-defense. But the doubter, in reply, will ask to what extent the cost even of a successful war of national defense—in life, money, material, foods, health, and (inevitably) freedom—may amount to a national defeat. National defense through war always involves some degree of national defeat. This paradox has been with us from the very beginning of our republic. Militarization in defense of freedom reduces the freedom of the defenders. There is a fundamental inconsistency between war and freedom.

The Contradictions of Modern Warfare

In a modern war, fought with modern weapons and on the modern scale, neither side can limit to "the enemy" the damage that it does. These wars damage the world. We know enough by now to know that you cannot damage a part of the world without damaging all of it. Modern war has not only made it impossible to kill "combatants" without killing "noncombatants," it has made it impossible to damage your enemy without damaging yourself.

That many have considered the increasing unacceptability of modern warfare is shown by the language of the propaganda surrounding it. Modern wars have characteristically been fought to end war; they have been fought in the name of peace. Our most terrible weapons have been made, ostensibly, to preserve and assure the peace of the world. "All we want is peace," we say as we increase relentlessly our capacity to make war.

Yet at the end of a century in which we have fought two wars to end war and several more to prevent war and preserve peace, and in which scientific and technological progress has made war ever more terrible and less controllable, we still, by policy, give no consideration to nonviolent means of national defense. We do indeed make much of diplomacy and diplomatic relations, but by diplomacy we mean invariably ultimatums for peace backed by the threat of war. It is always understood that we stand ready to kill those with whom we are "peacefully negotiating."

Our century of war, militarism, and political terror has produced great—and successful—advocates of true peace, among whom Mohandas Gandhi and Martin Luther King, Jr., are the paramount examples. The considerable success that they achieved testifies to the presence, in the midst of violence, of an authentic and powerful desire for peace and, more important, of the proven will to make the necessary sacrifices. But so far as our government is concerned, these men and their great and authenticating accomplishments might as well never have existed. To achieve peace by peaceable means is not yet our goal. We cling to the hopeless paradox of making peace by making war.

A Brutal Hypocrisy

Which is to say that we cling in our public life to a brutal hypocrisy. In our century of almost universal violence of humans against fellow humans, and against our natural and cultural commonwealth, hypocrisy has been inescapable because our opposition to violence has been selective or merely fashionable. Some of us who approve of our monstrous military budget and our peacekeeping wars nonetheless deplore "domestic violence" and think that our society can be pacified by "gun control." Some of us are against capital punishment but for abortion. Some of us are against abortion but for capital punishment.

War Is Never Justified

Kings, rulers, ministers, and governments often fall back on war as a crude means to their ends. This reflects a lack of intelligence, creativity, and courage in solving problems. The ends, even when decent and just, never justify the violence of war.

War is never peace.

Santikaro Bhikkhu, Buddhist Peace Fellowship, www.bpf.org, 2003.

One does not have to know very much or think very far in order to see the moral absurdity upon which we have erected our sanctioned enterprises of violence. Abortion-as-birth-control is justified as a "right," which can establish itself only by denying all the rights of another person, which is the most primitive intent of warfare. Capital punishment sinks us all to the same level of primal belligerence, at which an act of violence is avenged by another act of violence.

What the justifiers of these acts ignore is the fact—well-established by the history of feuds, let alone the history of war—that violence breeds violence. Acts of violence committed in "justice" or in affirmation of "rights" or in defense of "peace" do not end violence. They prepare and justify its continuation.

Dangerous Absurdities

The most dangerous superstition of the parties of violence is the idea that sanctioned violence can prevent or control unsanctioned violence. But if violence is "just" in one instance as determined by the state, why might it not also be "just" in another instance, as determined by an individual? How can a society that justifies capital punishment and warfare prevent its justifications from being extended to assassination and terrorism? If a government perceives that some causes are so important as to justify the killing of children, how can it hope to prevent the contagion of its logic spreading to its citizens—or to its citizens' children?

If we give to these small absurdities the magnitude of international relations, we produce, unsurprisingly, some much larger absurdities. What could be more absurd, to begin with, than our attitude of high moral outrage against other nations for manufacturing the selfsame weapons that we manufacture? The difference, as our leaders say, is that we will use these weapons virtuously, whereas our enemies will use them maliciously—a proposition that too readily conforms to a proposition of much less dignity: we will use them in our interest, whereas our enemies will use them in theirs.

Or we must say, at least, that the issue of virtue in war is as obscure, ambiguous, and troubling as Abraham Lincoln found to be the issue of prayer in war: "Both [the North and the South] read the same bible, and pray to the same God, and each invokes his aid against the other. . . . The prayers of both could not be answered—that of neither could be answered fully."

Keeping War at a Distance

Recent American wars, having been both "foreign" and "limited," have been fought under the assumption that little or no personal sacrifice is required. In "foreign" wars, we do not directly experience the damage that we inflict upon the enemy. We hear and see this damage reported in the news, but we are not affected. These limited, "foreign" wars require that some of our young people should be killed or crippled, and that some families should grieve, but these "casualties" are so widely distributed among our population as hardly to be noticed.

Otherwise, we do not feel ourselves to be involved. We pay taxes to support the war, but that is nothing new, for we pay war taxes also in time of "peace." We experience no shortages, we suffer no rationing, we endure no limitations. We earn, borrow, spend, and consume in wartime as in peacetime.

And of course no sacrifice is required of those large economic interests that now principally constitute our economy. No corporation will be required to submit to any limitation or to sacrifice a dollar. On the contrary, war is the great cure-all and opportunity of our corporate economy, which subsists and thrives upon war. War ended the Great Depression of the 1930s, and we have maintained a war economy—an economy, one might justly say, of general violence—ever since, sacrificing to it an enormous economic and ecological wealth, including, as designated victims, the farmers and the industrial working class.

And so great costs are involved in our fixation on war, but the costs are "externalized" as "acceptable losses." And here we see how progress in war, progress in technology, and progress in the industrial economy are parallel to one another—or, very often, are merely identical.

A Suspicious Accounting

Romantic nationalists, which is to say most apologists for war, always imply in their public speeches a mathematics or an accounting of war. Thus by its suffering in the Civil War, the North is said to have "paid for" the emancipation of the slaves and the preservation of the Union. Thus we may speak of our liberty as having been "bought" by the bloodshed of patriots. I am fully aware of the truth in such statements. I know that I am one of many who have benefited from painful sacrifices made by other people, and I would not like to be ungrateful. Moreover, I am a patriot myself and I know that the time may come for any of us when we must make extreme sacrifices for the sake of liberty—a fact confirmed by the fates of Gandhi and King.

But still I am suspicious of this kind of accounting. For one reason, it is necessarily done by the living on behalf of the dead. And I think we must be careful about too easily accepting, or being too easily grateful for, sacrifices made by others, especially if we have made none ourselves. For another reason, though our leaders in war always assume that there is an acceptable price, there is never a previously stated level of acceptability. The acceptable price, finally, is whatever is paid.

It is easy to see the similarity between this accounting of the price of war and our usual accounting of "the price of progress." We seem to have agreed that whatever has been (or will be) paid for so-called progress is an acceptable price. If that price includes the diminishment of privacy and the increase of government secrecy, so be it. If it means a radical reduction in the number of small businesses and the virtual destruction of the farm population, so be it. If it means the devastation of whole regions by extractive industries, so be it. If it means that a mere handful of people should own more billions of wealth than is owned by all of the world's poor, so be it.

Waging Economic Warfare

But let us have the candor to acknowledge that what we call "the economy" or "the free market" is less and less distinguishable from warfare. For about half of the last century, we worried about world conquest by international communism. Now with less worry (so far) we are witnessing world conquest by international capitalism.

Though its political means are milder (so far) than those of communism, this newly internationalized capitalism may prove even more destructive of human cultures and communities, of freedom, and of nature. Its tendency is just as much toward total dominance and control. Confronting this conquest, ratified and licensed by the new international trade agreements, no place and no community in the world may consider itself safe from some form of plunder. More and more people all over the world are recognizing that this is so, and they are saying that world conquest of any kind is wrong, period.

They are doing more than that. They are saying that local conquest also is wrong, and wherever it is taking place local people are joining together to oppose it. All over my own state of Kentucky this opposition is growing—from the west, where the exiled people of the Land Between the Lakes are struggling to save their homeland from bureaucratic depredation, to the east, where the native people of the mountains are still struggling to preserve their land from destruction by absentee corporations.

To have an economy that is warlike, that aims at conquest and that destroys virtually everything that it is dependent on, placing no value on the health of nature or of human communities, is absurd enough. It is even more absurd that this economy, that in some respects is so much at one with our military industries and programs, is in other respects directly in conflict with our professed aim of national defense.

Squandering Resources

It seems only reasonable, only sane, to suppose that a gigantic program of preparedness for national defense should be founded first of all upon a principle of national and even regional economic independence. A nation determined to defend itself and its freedoms should be prepared, and always preparing, to live from its own resources and from the work and the skills of its own people. But that is not what we are doing in the United States today. What we are doing is squandering in the most prodigal manner the natural and human resources of the nation.

At present, in the face of declining finite sources of fossil fuel energies, we have virtually no energy policy, either for conservation or for the development of safe and clean alternative sources. At present, our energy policy simply is to use all that we have. Moreover, in the face of a growing population needing to be fed, we have virtually no policy for land conservation and no policy of just compensation to the primary producers of food. Our agricultural policy is to use up everything that we have, while depending increasingly on imported food, energy, technology, and labor.

Those are just two examples of our general indifference to our own needs. We thus are elaborating a surely dangerous contradiction between our militant nationalism and our espousal of the international "free market" ideology. How do we escape from this absurdity?

I don't think there is an easy answer. Obviously, we would be less absurd if we took better care of things. We would be less absurd if we founded our public policies upon an honest description of our needs and our predicament, rather than upon fantastical descriptions of our wishes. We would be less absurd if our leaders would consider in good faith the proven alternatives to violence.

Such things are easy to say, but we are disposed, somewhat by culture and somewhat by nature, to solve our problems by violence, and even to enjoy doing so. And yet by now all of us must at least have suspected that our right to live, to be free, and to be at peace is not guaranteed by any act of violence. It can be guaranteed only by our willingness that all other persons should live, be free, and be at peace—and by our willingness to use or give our own lives to make that possible. To be incapable of such willingness is merely to resign ourselves to the absurdity we are in; and yet, if you are like me, you are unsure to what extent you are capable of it.

Here is the other question that I have been leading toward, one that the predicament of modern warfare forces upon us: How many deaths of other people's children by bombing or starvation are we willing to accept in order that we may be free, affluent, and (supposedly) at peace? To that question I answer: None. Please, no children. Don't kill any children for my benefit.

If that is your answer too, then you must know that we have not come to rest, far from it. For surely we must feel ourselves swarmed about with more questions that are urgent, personal, and intimidating. But perhaps also we feel ourselves beginning to be free, facing at last in our own selves the greatest challenge ever laid before us, the most comprehensive vision of human progress, the best advice, and the least obeyed:

Love your enemies, bless them that curse you, do good to them that hate you, and pray for them which despitefully use you and persecute you; That ye may be the children of your Father which is in heaven: for he maketh his sun to rise on the evil and the good, and sendeth rain on the just and on the unjust.

"Winning [the war against terrorism] may require the use of preemptive force against terrorist forces as well as against the states that harbor them."

Preemptive War Is Sometimes Justified

Michael J. Glennon

In the following viewpoint Michael J. Glennon argues that preemptive war is sometimes justified to deter potential attacks. Glennon claims that international laws that reject the use of force except in self-defense are outdated and do not protect against twenty-first-century enemies such as terrorists and rogue nations with weapons of mass destruction. The fact that a majority of United Nations members have resorted to preemptive war further supports its use, he maintains. Glennon, a fellow at the Woodrow Wilson International Center for Scholars in Washington, D.C., is professor of law at the University of California, Davis, and author of *Limits of Law, Prerogatives of Power: Interventionism After Kosovo.*

As you read, consider the following questions:

1. What does Article 51 of the UN Charter state, as cited by Glennon?
2. In the author's opinion, in what five ways have security needs changed since 1945?
3. According to the author, what are the dangers of preemptive force?

Michael J. Glennon, "Preempting Terrorism: The Case for Anticipatory Self-Defense," *The Weekly Standard*, vol. 7, January 28, 2002, pp. 24–27. Copyright © 2002 by News Corporation, Weekly Standard. All rights reserved. Reproduced by permission.

The Bush Doctrine, as promulgated by President Bush following the September 11, 2001 [terrorist attacks on America], contemplates preemptive use of force against terrorists as well as the states that harbor them. If the United Nations Charter is to be believed, however, carrying out that doctrine would be unlawful: The Charter permits use of force by states only in response to an armed attack. In 1945, when the Charter was framed, this prohibition against anticipatory self-defense may have seemed realistic. Today, it is not. Indeed, it is no longer binding law.

The Right of Self-Defense

Since time immemorial, the use of force has been permitted in self-defense in the international as well as all domestic legal systems, and for much the same reason: With states as with individuals, the most elemental right is survival. So powerful has been its claim that the right of self-defense was considered implicit in earlier treaties limiting use of force by states; the Kellogg-Briand Peace Pact of 1928, like the 1919 Covenant of the League of Nations, made no mention of it.

In 1945, the right was made explicit. Article 51 of the United Nations Charter states expressly: "Nothing in the present Charter shall impair the inherent right of individual or collective self-defense if an armed attack occurs against a Member of the United Nations. . . ." Self-defense thus emerged as the sole purpose under the Charter for which states may use force without Security Council approval.

While the Charter professes not to "impair" the inherent right to self-defense, it does precisely that. Prior to 1945, states used defensive force *before* an attack had occurred, to *forestall* an attack. The plain language of Article 51 permits defensive use of force only *if* an armed attack occurs. If none has occurred, defensive force—"anticipatory self-defense"—is not permitted.

This new impairment of the right of self-defense was widely seen as sensible when the Charter was adopted. States had often used the claim of self-defense as a pretext for aggression. (The Nazi defendants at Nuremberg argued that Germany had attacked the Soviet Union, Norway, and Denmark in self-defense, fearing that Germany was about to be attacked.)

If profligate use of force was ever to be reined in, narrower limits had to be imposed. And those limits had to be set out with a bright line; qualifying defensive rights with words like "reasonable," "imminent," or even "necessary" would leave states too much discretion and too much room for abuse. The occurrence of an actual armed attack was thus set up as an essential predicate for the use of force. The new requirement narrowed significantly the circumstances in which force could be used. And it set out a readily identifiable and, it was thought, objectively verifiable event to trigger defensive rights. Phony defensive justifications would be less plausible and war would be less frequent, thereby vindicating the first great purpose of the Charter—"to maintain international peace and security."

The impairment was realistic, it was further thought, because the need for anticipatory defense would diminish. The reason was that the UN Security Council would pick up where individual states were now compelled by the Charter to leave off. The Council, to be equipped with its own standing or standby forces, was authorized to use force in response to any "threat to the peace"—authority far broader than that accorded individual states. Coupled with the requirement that states report to the Security Council when using defensive force, this new institution—this "constabulary power before which barbaric and atavistic forces will stand in awe," as [British Prime Minister Winston] Churchill described it—would make anticipatory self-help a thing of the past.

All know that it didn't work out that way. Throughout the Cold War the Security Council deadlocked repeatedly on security issues. States never gave the Council the peace enforcement troops contemplated by the Charter's framers. The Council authorized (rather than used) force only haphazardly "to maintain or restore international peace and security." And, as discussed later, states continued to use force often, obviously not in response to armed attacks.

Moving Beyond Conventional Justifications

Still, like most states, the United States never formally claimed a right to anticipatory self-defense—i.e., to use armed force absent an armed attack, so as to prevent one from occurring.

During the 1962 Cuban Missile Crisis, the United States declined to rely upon Article 51, claiming instead that the "quarantine" of Cuba was authorized by the Organization of American States (and implicitly by the Security Council). When Israel seemed to assert a right to use defensive force to prevent an imminent Arab attack in June 1967, and even when Israel squarely claimed that right in attacking an Iraqi nuclear reactor in 1981, the United States steered clear of the issue of anticipatory self-defense. In 1986, however, the United States finally did claim the right to use "preemptive" force against Libya following the bombing of a Berlin night club that killed two Americans.

This last incident is worth considering closely: The Libyan bombing highlights the doctrinal confusion surrounding self-defense and also marks a proverbial "paradigm shift" in American thinking on the question. Why insist upon an actual armed attack as a precondition for the use of force? The axiomatic answer, under long-standing dogma, is of course that force is necessary to protect against the attack. But by acknowledging that its use of force against Libya was preemptive, the United States in effect moved beyond the conventional justification. The Berlin bombing was obviously over and finished; no use of force was, or conceivably could have been, instrumental in "defending" Americans killed at the Berlin club. The United States was not, in this sense, responding *defensively*. It was engaged in a forward-looking action, an action directed at future, not past, attacks on Americans. Its use of force against Libya was triggered by the Berlin attack only in the sense that that attack was *evidence of the threat of future attacks*. Evidence of Libyan capabilities and intentions sufficient to warrant preemptive force might well have taken (and, in fact, also did take) the form of intelligence reports. From a purely epistemological standpoint, no actual armed attack was necessary.

Discouraging Future Attacks

Although the United States did not spell out its thinking this explicitly, in later incidents it acted on precisely this future-looking rationale. True, the United States was in each instance able to argue that actual armed attacks had occurred.

But in each of those subsequent incidents, the United States was *responding to evidence of future intent and capability*, not defending against past action. Its objective was to avert future attacks through preemption and deterrence.

In 1993, for example, the United States fired cruise missiles at the Iraqi intelligence headquarters in Baghdad following an alleged effort by Iraq to assassinate President George Bush. But the assassination attempt was long since over; the United States used force not to defend against illicit force already deployed, but to discourage such force from being deployed in the future. In 1998, the United States fired cruise missiles at a terrorist training camp in Afghanistan and a pharmaceutical plant in Sudan following attacks on U.S. embassies in Kenya and Tanzania. Again, the provocation had ended; in no way can the United States be seen as having defended itself against the specific armed attack to which its embassies had been subject.

So, too, with the use of force against Afghanistan following September 11. The armed attack against the World Trade Center and the Pentagon was over, and no defensive action could have ameliorated its effects. The U.S. use of force was prompted by the threat of future attacks. And it was evidence of that threat—gleaned from multiple intelligence sources, not simply from the September 11 attack—to which the United States responded with its action against Afghanistan. That action could well have been warranted even if September 11 had never occurred. The problem lay in the future, not the past.

Preemption and Deterrence

In each of these incidents, the United States justified its action under Article 51 of the Charter, claiming to be engaged in the *defensive* use of force. But in fact something different was going on. In each incident, the United States was—as it acknowledged forthrightly following the 1986 bombing of Libya—engaged in the use of *preemptive* force. The two are not the same. The justification for genuine defensive force was set forth by U.S. Secretary of State Daniel Webster in the famous *Caroline* case of 1837. To use it, he wrote, a state must "show a necessity of self-defense, instant, overwhelming, leaving no choice of means, and no moment of deliberation." (This formula continues to be widely cited by states, tribunals, and commentators as part and parcel of the law of the Charter.) Obviously, in none of the incidents canvassed above can the American use of force be said to meet the *Caroline* standard. None of the American armed responses needed to be, or was, instant. In each the United States deliberated for weeks or months before responding, carefully choosing its means. Those means were directed not at *defending against* an attack that had already begun, but at *preempting*, or *deterring*, an attack that *could* begin at some point in the future.

Preemptive War Is Just War

Over the centuries, the criteria for a just war have been established mainly through Christian theology and are firmly rooted in Holy Scripture. A just war has to be defensive—waged as a last resort—to secure justice, remedy injustice, protect the innocent or champion human rights. It must follow a formal declaration and be undertaken with a reasonable expectation of success.

For a war to be just, it must target only enemy combatants and be proportionate while it's being waged so it does not inflict damage greater than the evil being redressed. There is nothing in these guidelines that prohibits a pre-emptive war.

Raymond J. Keating, *New York Newsday*, March 12, 2004.

In fact, the United States had long ago accepted the logic of using armed force without waiting to be attacked. In the early 1960s, President John F. Kennedy seriously considered launching a preemptive strike against the People's Republic of China to prevent it from developing nuclear weapons. In 1994, President Bill Clinton contemplated a preemptive attack against North Korea for the same reason. During the Cold War, the United States retained the option of launching its nuclear weapons upon warning that a nuclear attack was about to occur—before the United States actually had been attacked—so as to protect command and control systems that were vulnerable to a Soviet first strike.

It thus came as no dramatic policy change when, in the Bush Doctrine, the United States publicly formalized its rejection of the armed attack requirement and officially announced its acceptance of preemption as a legitimate rationale for the use of force. "Every nation now knows," President George W. Bush said on December 11 [2001], "that we cannot accept—and we will not accept—states that harbor, finance, train, or equip the agents of terror."

A Different World

That formalization was overdue. Twenty-first-century security needs are different from those imagined in San Francisco in 1945.

First, as noted above, the intended safeguard against unlawful threats of force—a vigilant and muscular Security Council—never materialized. Self-help is the only realistic alternative.

Second, modern methods of intelligence collection, such as satellite imagery and communications intercepts, now make it unnecessary to sit out an actual armed attack to await convincing proof of a state's hostile intent.

Third, with the advent of weapons of mass destruction and their availability to international terrorists, the first blow can be devastating—far more devastating than the pinprick attacks on which the old rules were premised.

Fourth, terrorist organizations "of global reach" were unknown when Article 51 was drafted. To flourish, they need to conduct training, raise money, and develop and stockpile weaponry—which in turn requires communications equipment, camps, technology, staffing, and offices. All this requires a sanctuary, which only states can provide—and which only states can take away.

Fifth, the danger of catalytic war erupting from the use of preemptive force has lessened with the end of the Cold War. It made sense to hew to Article 51 during the Cuban Missile Crisis, when two nuclear superpowers confronted each other toe-to-toe. It makes less sense today, when safe-haven states and terrorist organizations are not themselves possessed of preemptive capabilities.

A Need for Caution

Still, it must be acknowledged that, at least in the short term, wider use of preemptive force could be destabilizing. The danger exists that some states threatened with preemptive action (consider India and Pakistan) will be all too ready to preempt probable preemptors. This is another variant of the quandary confronted when states, in taking steps to enhance their security, unintentionally threaten the security of adversaries—and thus find their own security diminished as adversaries take compensatory action.

But the way out of the dilemma, here as elsewhere, is not underreaction and concession. The way out lies in the adoption of prudent defensive strategies calculated to meet reasonably foreseeable security threats that pose a common danger. Such strategies generate community support and cause adversaries to adapt perceptions and, ultimately, to recalibrate their intentions and capabilities. That process can take time, during which the risk of greater systemic instability must be weighed against the risk of worldwide terrorist attacks of increased frequency and magnitude.

The greater danger is not long-term instability but the possibility that use of preemptive force could prove incomplete or ineffective. It is not always possible to locate all maleficent weapons or facilities, thereby posing the risk that some will survive a preemptive strike and be used in retaliation. Similarly, if a rogue state such as Iraq considers itself the likely target of preemptive force, its leaders may have an incentive to defend with weapons of mass destruction—weapons they would not otherwise use—in the belief that they have nothing to lose. A reliable assessment of likely costs is an essential precondition to any preemptive action.

Weighing the Options

These are the sorts of considerations that policymakers must weigh in deciding whether to use preemptive force. Preemption obviously is a complement, not a stand-alone alternative, to non-coercive policy options. When available, those options normally are preferable. The point here is simply that preemption is a legitimate option, and that—the language of the Charter notwithstanding—preemption is lawful. States can no longer be said to regard the Charter's rules concerning anticipatory self-defense—or concerning the use of force in general, for that matter—as binding. The question—the sole question, in the consent-based international legal system—is whether states have in fact agreed to be bound by the Charter's use-of-force rules. If states had truly intended to make those rules obligatory, they would have made the cost of violation greater than the perceived benefits.

They have not. The Charter's use-of-force rules have been widely and regularly disregarded. Since 1945, two-thirds of the members of the United Nations—126 states out of 189—have fought 291 interstate conflicts in which over 22 million people have been killed. In every one of those conflicts, at least one belligerent necessarily violated the Charter. In most of those conflicts, most of the belligerents claimed to act in self-defense. States' earlier intent, expressed in words, has been superseded by their later intent, expressed in deeds.

Rather, therefore, than split legal hairs about whether a given use of force is an armed reprisal, intervention, armed attack, aggression, forcible countermeasure, or something else in international law's over-schematized catalogue of misdeeds, American policymakers are well advised to attend directly to protecting the safety and well-being of the American people. For fifty years, despite repeated efforts, the international community has been unable to agree on when the use of force is lawful and when it is not. There will be plenty of time to resume that discussion when the war on terrorism is won. If the "barbaric and atavistic" forces succeed, however, there will be no point in any such discussion, for the law of the jungle will prevail. Completing that victory is the task at hand. And winning may require the use of pre-emptive force against terrorist forces as well as against the states that harbor them.

> *"This doctrine of preemption would invite any state to attack any adversary that it perceived was threatening it."*

Preemptive War Cannot Be Justified

Charles W. Kegley Jr. and Gregory A. Raymond

Accepting the use of preemptive strikes will increase wars worldwide, claim Charles W. Kegley Jr. and Gregory A. Raymond in the following viewpoint. When the United States, a world leader, justifies preemptive strikes against enemies it considers a threat, other nations will follow, making the world less safe. Preemptive strikes violate long-standing international rules of war that have been vital in enhancing global security, they maintain. Kegley, a *USA Today* editor and professor of international relations, is author of *The Nuclear Reader: Strategy, Weapons, War.* Raymond is author of *Conflict Resolution and the Structure of the State System.*

As you read, consider the following questions:

1. According to the authors, why are terrorist threats more real in the age of globalization?
2. In the authors' opinion, what was the cost to Rome in the preventive war against Carthage in 146 B.C.?
3. Why did international law not break down under the prevailing norm that justified war making prior to the terrorist attacks of September 11, 2001, in the authors' view?

In the immediate aftermath of the terrorist attacks on September 11, 2001, the U.S. began a war against global terrorism. Soon thereafter, America abandoned its Cold War strategy of containment, embracing the doctrine of preemptive warfare aimed at attacking suspected aggressors before they could strike first. This, in turn, led to the invasion of Iraq in March, 2003.

The Bush Administration's doctrine of preempting terrorists and rogue states, in what is called alternatively "forward deterrence" or "anticipatory self-defense," raises anew timeless moral and legal issues about the conditions under which, and purposes for which, a just war for self-defense is permissible to counter a threat to national security. What it has advanced as a new national security strategy is nothing less than an amputation of the normative pillar on which global society has been based at least since 1928, when the Kellogg-Briand pact outlawed war as an instrument of foreign policy. This radical revision of customary international law is leading the world into uncharted waters. If it becomes permissible to attack other international actors who do not pose an imminent threat, then, without a moral principle to guide international conduct, war is likely to increase.

The Signs of Change

President [George W.] Bush first signaled the policy change he was initiating on June 1, 2002, at West Point. To his way of thinking, 9/11 created unprecedented "new deadly challenges" that necessitated new approaches and rules for statecraft. Chastising tyrants like Iraq's Saddam Hussein as international outlaws, the President announced that "We must be prepared to stop rogue states and their terrorist clients before they are able to threaten or use weapons of mass destruction against the United States and our allies and friends. . . . Traditional concepts of deterrence will not work against a terrorist enemy whose avowed tactics are wanton destruction and the targeting of innocents, whose so-called soldiers seek martyrdom in death. . . . The greater the threat, the greater the risk of inaction—and the more compelling the case for taking anticipatory action to defend ourselves, even if uncertainty remains as to the time and place of the enemy's attack. To forestall or prevent such hostile acts by our adversaries, the United States will, if necessary, act preemptively."

This reasoning soon thereafter became the cornerstone of The National Security Strategy of the United States of America (NSS), released on September 17 [2002]. It reiterated Bush's West Point declaration that the era of deterrence was over and preemption was an idea whose time had come. It then proceeded to assert that, "Given the goals of rogue states and terrorists, the United States can no longer solely rely on a reactive posture as we have in the past. . . . We cannot let our enemies strike first." The NSS added, "Nations need not suffer an attack before they can lawfully take action to defend themselves against forces that present an imminent danger of attack."

Opening the Floodgates

The extreme revisionism of the Bush doctrine undercuts a key preemptory norm in international law that underpins all others—the use of force cannot be justified merely on account of an adversary's capabilities, but solely in defense against its aggressive actions. Preemption represents a frontal rejection of Articles 2 (4) and 51 of the United Nations Charter that condones war only in self-defense. It opens the door to military first strikes against adversaries, under the claim that their motives are evil and that they are building the military capabilities to inflict mass destruction.

It is not difficult to appreciate the grave dangers that have prompted this watershed in U.S. national strategy. The threats which provoked the President's extreme strategic response are real. Raison d'etat dictates that actions be taken for the preservation of the state, and, in these threatening circumstances, many find reasonable the claim that the national interest makes such countermeasures imperative. The temptation to attack first an adversary who might attack you is, of course, often overwhelming. Why stand by in the face of a potential threat? "An ounce of prevention is worth a pound of cure," a popular cliche advises. Better to hit an enemy before it attacks, than to be left prostrate. . . .

That realpolitik logic was at the root of the NSS proposition that the "best defense is a good offense," and the premise behind the President's explanation in an October 7, 2002, speech in Cincinnati that "We have every reason to assume the worst, and we have an urgent duty to prevent the worst from happening." A proactive policy through preemption is defined as necessary because it was argued that America "cannot wait for the final proof—the smoking gun—that could come in the form of a mushroom cloud."

Rall. © 2004 by Universal Press Syndicate. Reproduced by permission.

Fear is a great motivator. There are ample reasons to fear terrorists like Osama bin Laden and tyrants like [Iraqi leader Saddam Hussein]. The threats are real in this age of globalization in which boundaries are no longer barriers to external threats, a suitcase nuclear bomb or a chemical/biological weapon can obliterate any American city, and a terrorist can strike anywhere and anytime. The U.S. is vulnerable, so there is an understandable compulsion to eliminate threats by any means available, including preemptive strikes.

From Preemption to Prevention

Preemption is advocated as a policy, but what must be understood is that this strategy goes beyond that goal to a whole other level—to preventive war. The Bush doctrine transcends the established limitations of the use of armed force in self-defense against a prior armed attack. "The President is not 'reserving a right' to respond to imminent threats," wrote Duke University professor of international relations Michael Byers in the July 25, 2002, issue of *The London Review of Books*, "he is seeking an extension of the fight of self-defense to include action against potential future dangers."

As the wording of the Bush NSS illuminates, the line between preemption and prevention is blurry. How does one distinguish intentions from capabilities? Because an adversary amasses arsenals of weapons, does that necessarily mean that those weapons are for aggression instead of defense? Without knowledge of motives, prudence dictates worst-case assumptions. This invites the so-called "security dilemma" that results when one country's arms acquisitions provokes corresponding actions by alarmed adversaries, with the result that all participants in the arms race experience reduced security as their weaponry increases. Preemption addresses the danger by attacking first and asking questions about intentions later.

The quest to redefine international rules to permit preemptive strikes has deeper philosophical, ethical, and legal consequences for the long term, beyond its unforeseen immediate impact. Does it threaten to weaken international security and, paradoxically, U.S. national security as well? To probe this question, let us look briefly at some historical precedents to preemptive practices in order to put the current policy into perspective. Consider some salient illustrations that precede Bush's rationale.

A History of Preemption

In the third Punic War fought between the Roman and Carthaginian empires (264–147 B.C.), after a 50-year hiatus, the Romans bought the advice of the 81-year-old Cato the Elder. Consumed with the fear that renewed Punic power would culminate eventually in Roman defeat unless drastic military measures were taken, he ended every speech to the Roman Senate by proclaiming "Carthaginian esse delendum" (Carthage must be destroyed). Heeding Cato's advice,

Rome launched a preventive war of annihilation and, in 146 B.C., some 500,000 Carthaginian citizens were destroyed in an act of mass genocide, and an entire civilization was obliterated. The foreign threat had been met; thereafter, no challenges to Roman hegemony existed—but at what cost? The Roman historian Polybius prophetically lamented, "I feel a terror and dread lest someone someday should give the same order about my own native city." Perhaps this led him to conclude that "it is not the object of war to annihilate those who have given provocation to it, but to cause them to mend their ways." Worse still, this preventive war can be said to have destroyed the soul of Rome. After it, Rome suffered a prolonged period of revolutionary strife, and much later found itself victim of the same savage preemptive measures by invaders it had once inflicted on Carthage. "Val victis" (Woe betide the defeated), the Romans cried after the city was sacked by the Gauls in 390 A.D. Is there an object lesson here? Read on.

December 7, 1941, was "a day that will live in infamy," a President Franklin D. Roosevelt declared in reaction to Japan's sneak attack on Pearl Harbor. That strike removed most of the U.S. Pacific fleet and thereby redressed the Japanese-American military balance of power. The attack was premeditated, for arguably preventive purposes—to hit the U.S. before it could use its superior military capabilities to smother Japanese imperialism and Japan's Asian Co-Prosperity Sphere in its cradle. However, preventive action hardly proved practical. It backfired, provoking the sleeping American giant from isolationistic neutrality into an angry wrath without restraint, leading to the annihilating atomic bombing of Hiroshima on August 6, 1945.

In June, 1981, Iraq was making rapid headway, with French assistance, toward building a nuclear reactor. Israeli warplanes destroyed that facility in a strike that prevented Iraq from acquiring nuclear weapons. The attack was planned, and, with pinpoint accuracy and effectiveness, the potential threat (that Prime Minister Menachem Begin regarded as the most-serious challenge to Israeli self-preservation) was removed. Begin, a former terrorist, undertook terrorism against a proven terrorist and tyrant, thus practicing the same strategy he sought to contain. As G. John Ikenberry, the Peter F. Krogh Professor of Geopolitics and Global Justice at Georgetown University, notes, this attack broke normative barriers, "and the world condemned it as an act of aggression"—as unjustifiable and shortsighted. The Reagan Administration condemned the strike; France pronounced it "unacceptable"; and Great Britain berated it as "a grave breach of international law." The strategy worked, however, in the short run, as Iraqi plans for cross-border attacks on Kuwait, Iran, and, in all likelihood, Israel were averted. In the long run, though, the preventive attack strengthened Saddam's grip on power at home and animated his military ambitions to try harder—in the name of defense.

The Excuses for War

History is thus replete with examples of states that have rationalized preemptive surgical attacks against a rival for preventive purposes. In fact, it is hard to find many cases of states that did not claim that, in initiating war, they were merely acting prudently in self-defense. Nearly all wars have been justified by that claim. This record suggests that preventive war is a problem, not a solution.

Bush asserts that, "If we wait for threats to fully materialize, we will have waited too long." That justification has been voiced by many before as an excuse for war. As *New York Times* columnist Bill Keller observes, historians cite as U.S. examples of preemptive interventions "Woodrow Wilson's occupation of Haiti in 1915, Lyndon Johnson's dispatch of U.S. Marines to the Dominican Republic in 1965, and Ronald Reagan's invasion of Grenada in 1983. [But] while preemption has been an occasional fact of life, [until George W. Bush] no president has so explicitly elevated the practice to a doctrine. Previous American leaders preferred to fabricate pretexts . . . rather than admit they were going in 'unprovoked.'"

The Risks of Preemptive Warfare

If a permissive climate of opinion on the acceptability of preemptive and preventive warfare takes root, will the U.S. and the world at large be safer and more secure? The normative barriers to the first-strike initiation of war vanish in a world in which preemption for prevention is accepted. Let us examine the blaring downside of the U.S. advocacy of preemptive warfare.

Preemption and its extension to preventive war is a direct challenge to prevailing norms. To encapsulate the international legal consensus prior to 9/11, before U.S. doctrine began to challenge it, one might say that international law over time had gravitated toward increasingly restrictive sets of rules for justified war making. Aggressive war was illegal, but defensive war was not. International law, therefore, did not break down whenever war broke out, for there are specified conditions under which states were permitted to wage a war. Those criteria were highly restrictive, though, confining war to serve as a penal method for punishing a prior attack by an aggressor.

How the U.S. chooses to act—its code of conduct—will be a powerful determinant of the rules followed throughout the international arena. Global leaders lead in creating the system's rules. When the reigning hegemon abandons an established rule and endorses a substitute one, the rules change for everyone. What the strongest do eventually defines what everybody should do, and when a practice becomes common it tends to be seen as obligatory. As Harvard University professor of international relations Stanley Hoffmann puts it, rules of behavior become rules for behavior. . . .

What the big powers do sets the standards that others follow. If other states act on the same rationale the U.S. has promulgated and take preventive military action against any enemy they claim is threatening them, the right to use force will be legitimized. The danger is that every country could conclude that preemption for preventive purposes is an acceptable practice. This doctrine of preemption would invite any state to attack any adversary that it perceived was threatening it.

A Bottomless Legal Pit

Perhaps unwittingly, the Bush Administration appears not to have taken into consideration the probability that its doctrine will encourage most others to accept that same doctrine, or that a bottomless legal pit will be created. "The specific doctrine of preemptive action," argues Ikenberry, "poses a problem: once the United States feels it can take such a course of action, nothing will stop other countries from doing the same." Indeed, that prophecy has already been fulfilled as others have emulated the American position by taking "up preemption as a way of dealing with these problems. The Bush doctrine—or at best the rhetoric—has already been appropriated by Russia against Georgia, by India against Pakistan. The dominoes can be expected to fall if the strategy of preemption continues to spread, as surely it will if the United States pursues its new policy." Or, as Keller opines, "If everyone embraces [the U.S.] new doctrine, a messy world would become a lot messier. Caveat pre-emptor."

If a permissive climate of opinion on the acceptability of preemptive and preventive warfare takes root, will the U.S. and the world at large be safer and more secure? That is doubtful. It has taken a long time for an international consensus to build behind the view that a preemptive attack to prevent an enemy's potential attack is outside the boundaries of justified warfare. In earlier epochs, states believed that they could attack another country for any reason deemed in the attacker's national interests. That climate of normative opinion has evaporated, and, partially as a consequence, the frequency of interstate war has steadily declined and almost vanished since the Cold War ended. Now, however, the U.S. has justified preemptive war under the claim that the benefits of preemption exceed the costs of acting only on retaliation for prior attacks for defense.

Inviting Emulation

This shift is not a cure; it is a curse. In pleading for preservation of the restrictive norms that prohibit preemptive strikes, historian Paul Schraeder, writing in *The American Conservative*, warns that the universal values "are changeable, fragile, gained only by great effort and through bitter lessons of history, and are easily destroyed, set aside, or changed for the worse for the sake of monetary gain or individual interest. And the fate of these norms and standards depends above all on what great powers, especially hegemons and superpowers do with them and to them. . . . The American example and standard for preemptive war, if carried out, would invite imitation and emulation, and get it. . . . A more dangerous, illegitimate norm and example can hardly be imagined. As could easily be shown by history, it completely subverts previous standards for judging the legitimacy of resorts to war, justifying any number of wars hitherto considered unjust and aggressive. [And] one can easily imagine plausible scenarios in which India could justly attack Pakistan or vice versa, or Israel or any one of its neighbors, or China [could attack] Taiwan, or South Korea [could attack] North Korea, under this rule that suspicion of what a hostile regime might do justifies launching preventive wars to overthrow it."

The Bush Administration has been vocal about the urgent need it perceives to do something about the dangers that confront U.S. security, but silent about the consequences that are likely to follow from that doctrinal shift to preemptive warfare. Do we really want to remove the normative handcuffs on the use of force? Do we really want to return to the freewheeling unrestricted sovereign right of any and all rulers to define for themselves when they are threatened, so as to license anticipatory preemptive warfare? Europe experimented with that Machiavellian basis for international statecraft in the 17th century during the deadly Thirty Years' War, which reduced its population by a third. Autonomy makes for global anarchy. Is severing normative anchors on permissible warfare that demonstrably have reduced its incidence really an idea that serves American and global interests and ideals? This radical departure in radical times looks increasingly like a path to peril and a road to ruin.

> *"Waging war is not only morally permitted, but morally necessary, as a response to calamitous acts of violence, hatred, and injustice."*

The War on Terror Is Justified

Institute for American Values

The following viewpoint, excerpted from a letter prepared by the Institute for American Values and signed by sixty scholars, argues that war is justified to stop terrorism. Although never to be used for aggressive purposes, war is morally justified to protect innocent people from extremists who violate the ethical principles that maintain orderly societies. The authors contend that terrorists now have access to weapons that can wreak enormous devastation and therefore pose a clear and present danger to innocent life worldwide. The Institute for American Values promotes policies that support marriage and family values.

As you read, consider the following questions:

1. What five fundamental truths do the authors maintain apply to all people?
2. In the authors' view, what are illegitimate reasons to fight wars?
3. In what way does the Islamic extremist movement betray fundamental Islamic principles, in the authors' opinion?

Institute for American Values, "What We're Fighting For: A Letter from America," www.americanvalues.org, February 2002. Copyright © 2002 by the Institute for American Values. Reproduced by permission.

At times it becomes necessary for a nation to defend itself through force of arms. Because war is a grave matter, involving the sacrifice and taking of precious human life, conscience demands that those who would wage the war state clearly the moral reasoning behind their actions, in order to make plain to one another, and to the world community, the principles they are defending.

Principles Worth Defending

We affirm five fundamental truths that pertain to all people without distinction:

1. All human beings are born free and equal in dignity and rights.
2. The basic subject of society is the human person, and the legitimate role of government is to protect and help to foster the conditions for human flourishing.
3. Human beings naturally desire to seek the truth about life's purpose and ultimate ends.
4. Freedom of conscience and religious freedom are inviolable rights of the human person.
5. Killing in the name of God is contrary to faith in God and is the greatest betrayal of the universality of religious faith.

We fight to defend ourselves and to defend these universal principles. . . .

A Necessary Response to Evil

We recognize that all war is terrible, representative finally of human political failure. We also know that the line separating good and evil does not run between one society and another, much less between one religion and another; ultimately, that line runs through the middle of every human heart. Finally, those of us—Jews, Christians, Muslims, and others—who are people of faith recognize our responsibility, stated in our holy scriptures, to love mercy and to do all in our power to prevent war and live in peace.

Yet reason and careful moral reflection also teach us that there are times when the first and most important reply to evil is to stop it. There are times when waging war is not only morally permitted, but morally necessary, as a response to calamitous acts of violence, hatred, and injustice. This is one of those times.

The idea of a "just war" is broadly based, with roots in many of the world's diverse religious and secular moral traditions. Jewish, Christian, and Muslim teachings, for example, all contain serious reflections on the definition of a just war. To be sure, some people, often in the name of realism, insist that war is essentially a realm of self-interest and necessity, making most attempts at moral analysis irrelevant. We disagree. Moral inarticulacy in the face of war is itself a moral stance—one that rejects the possibility of reason, accepts normlessness in international affairs, and capitulates to cynicism. To seek to apply objective moral reasoning to war is to defend the possibility of civil society and a world community based on justice.

Examining the Principles of Just War

The principles of just war teach us that wars of aggression and aggrandizement are never acceptable. Wars may not legitimately be fought for national glory, to avenge past wrongs, for territorial gain, or for any other non-defensive purpose.

The primary moral justification for war is to protect the innocent from certain harm. Augustine, whose early 5th century book, *The City of God*, is a seminal contribution to just war thinking, argues (echoing Socrates) that it is better for the Christian as an individual to suffer harm rather than to commit it. But is the morally responsible person also required, or even permitted, to make for *other* innocent persons a commitment to non-self-defense? For Augustine, and for the broader just war tradition, the answer is no. If one has compelling evidence that innocent people who are in no position to protect themselves will be grievously harmed unless coercive force is used to stop an aggressor, then the moral principle of love of neighbor calls us to the use of force.

Wars may not legitimately be fought against dangers that are small, questionable, or of uncertain consequence, or against dangers that might plausibly be mitigated solely through negotiation, appeals to reason, persuasion from third parties, or other nonviolent means. But if the danger to innocent life is real and certain, and especially if the aggressor is motivated by implacable hostility—if the end he seeks is not your willingness to negotiate or comply, but rather your destruction—then a resort to proportionate force is morally justified.

A just war can only be fought by a legitimate authority with responsibility for public order. Violence that is free-lance, opportunistic, or individualistic is never morally acceptable.

A just war can only be waged against persons who are combatants. Just war authorities from across history and around the world—whether they be Muslim, Jewish, Christian, from other faith traditions, or secular—consistently teach us that noncombatants are immune from deliberate attack. Thus, killing civilians for revenge, or even as a means of deterring aggression from people who sympathize with them, is morally wrong. Although in some circumstances, and within strict limits, it can be morally justifiable to undertake military actions that may result in the unintended but foreseeable death or injury of some noncombatants, it is not morally acceptable to make the killing of noncombatants the operational objective of a military action.

These and other just war principles teach us that, whenever human beings contemplate or wage war, it is both possible and necessary to affirm the sanctity of human life and embrace the principle of equal human dignity. These principles strive to preserve and reflect, even in the tragic activity of war, the fundamental moral truth that "others"—those who are strangers to us, those who differ from us in race or language, those whose religions we may believe to be untrue—have the same right to life that we do, and the same human dignity and human rights that we do.

A Violent, Extremist Movement

On September 11, 2001, a group of individuals deliberately attacked the United States, using highjacked airplanes as weapons with which to kill in less than two hours over 3,000 of our citizens in New York City, southwestern Pennsylvania, and Washington, D.C. Overwhelmingly, those who died on September 11 were civilians, not combatants, and were not known at all, except as Americans, by those who killed them.

Those who died on the morning of September 11 were killed unlawfully, wantonly, and with premeditated malice—a kind of killing that, in the name of precision, can only be described as murder. Those murdered included people from all races, many ethnicities, most major religions. They included dishwashers and corporate executives.

A Call to Action

No cause justifies the murder of innocent people. We totally reject terrorists and terrorism. We must rid the civilized world of this cancer. We must wage our campaign at every level, with every tool of statecraft, for as long as it takes.

President [George W.] Bush has stressed that, quote, "we will win this conflict by the patient accumulation of successes, by meeting a series of challenges with determination and will and purpose.". . .

This war has many fronts, from money laundering and the illicit drug trade, to arms trafficking and the proliferation of weapons of mass destruction. We must fight terrorism on all of these fronts.

Secretary of State Colin Powell, speech to the United Nations Security Council, January 20, 2003.

The individuals who committed these acts of war did not act alone, or without support, or for unknown reasons. They were members of an international Islamicist network, active in as many as 40 countries, now known to the world as Al Qaeda. This group, in turn, constitutes but one arm of a larger radical Islamicist movement, growing for decades and in some instances tolerated and even supported by governments, that openly professes its desire and increasingly demonstrates its ability to use murder to advance its objectives.

We use the terms "Islam" and "Islamic" to refer to one of the world's great religions, with about 1.2 billion adherents, including several million U.S. citizens, some of whom were murdered on September 11. It ought to go without saying—but we say it here once, clearly—that the great majority of the world's Muslims, guided in large measure by the teachings of the Qur'an [Koran], are decent, faithful, and peaceful. We use the terms "Islamicism" and "radical Islamicist" to refer to the violent, extremist, and radically intolerant religious-political movement that now threatens the world, including the Muslim world.

This radical, violent movement opposes not only certain U.S. and western policies—some signatories to this letter also oppose some of those policies—but also a foundational principle of the modern world, religious tolerance, as well as those fundamental human rights, in particular freedom of conscience and religion, that are enshrined in the United Nations Universal Declaration of Human Rights, and that must be the basis of any civilization oriented to human flourishing, justice, and peace.

This extremist movement claims to speak for Islam, but betrays fundamental Islamic principles. Islam sets its face *against* moral atrocities. For example, reflecting the teaching of the Qur'an and the example of the Prophet [Muhammad], Muslim scholars through the centuries have taught that struggle in the path of God (i.e., *jihad*) forbids the deliberate killing of noncombatants, and requires that military action be undertaken only at the behest of legitimate public authorities. They remind us forcefully that Islam, no less than Christianity, Judaism and other religions, is threatened and potentially degraded by these profaners who invoke God's name to kill indiscriminately.

We recognize that movements claiming the mantle of religion also have complex political, social, and demographic dimensions, to which due attention must be paid. At the same time, philosophy matters, and the animating philosophy of this radical Islamicist movement, in its contempt for human life, and by viewing the world as a life-and-death struggle between believers and unbelievers (whether nonradical Muslims, Jews, Christians, Hindus, or others), clearly denies the equal dignity of all persons and, in doing so, betrays religion and rejects the very foundation of civilized life and the possibility of peace among nations.

A Clear and Present Danger

Most seriously of all, the mass murders of September 11 demonstrated, arguably for the first time, that this movement now possesses not only the openly stated desire, but also the capacity and expertise—including possible access to, and willingness to use, chemical, biological and nuclear weapons—to wreak massive, horrific devastation on its intended targets.

Those who slaughtered more than 3,000 persons on September 11 and who, by their own admission, want nothing more than to do it again, constitute a clear and present danger to all people of good will everywhere in the world, not just the United States. Such acts are a pure example of naked aggression against innocent human life, a world-threatening evil that clearly requires the use of force to remove it.

Organized killers with global reach now threaten all of us. In the name of universal human morality, and fully conscious of the restrictions and requirements of a just war, we support our government's, and our society's, decision to use force of arms against them.

We pledge to do all we can to guard against the harmful temptations—especially those of arrogance and jingoism—to which nations at war so often seem to yield. At the same time, with one voice we say solemnly that it is crucial for our nation and its allies to win this war. We fight to defend ourselves, but we also believe that we fight to defend those universal principles of human rights and human dignity that are the best hope for humankind.

One day, this war will end. When it does—and in some respects even before it ends—the great task of conciliation awaits us. We hope that this war, by stopping an unmitigated global evil, can increase the possibility of a world community based on justice. But we know that only the peacemakers among us in every society can ensure that this war will not have been in vain.

We wish especially to reach out to our brothers and sisters in Muslim societies. We say to you forthrightly: We are not enemies, but friends. We must not be enemies. We have so much in common. There is so much that we must do together. Your human dignity, no less than ours—your rights and opportunities for a good life, no less than ours—are what we believe we're fighting for. We know that, for some of you, mistrust of us is high, and we know that we Americans are partly responsible for that mistrust. But we must not be enemies. In hope, we wish to join with you and all people of good will to build a just and lasting peace.

"You can call your war just . . . but that won't make it so."

The War on Terror Is Not Justified

Tim Wise

According to Tim Wise in the following viewpoint, America's war on terrorism is not justified because it will not reduce terrorism. In fact, Wise maintains, such violence, especially in Afghanistan, one of the poorest nations on earth, will only fuel anti-Americanism, which will lead to more terrorism against the United States. Wise is a writer, activist, and antiracism educator.

As you read, consider the following questions:
1. According to Wise, how has al Qaeda shown its respect for force?
2. In the author's view, did the United States effectively try peace in Afghanistan?
3. Why are food drops in Afghanistan insufficient, in the author's opinion?

Tim Wise, "Who's Being Naïve? War-Time Realism Through the Looking Glass," *Z Magazine*, October 28, 2001. Copyright © 2001 by *Z Magazine*. Reproduced by permission.

To hear those who support the . . . air assault on Afghanistan [in 2001] tell it, those of us who doubt the likely efficacy of such a campaign, and who question its fundamental morality are not only insufficiently patriotic but dangerously naïve.[1]

Lampooning the left for adhering to such ostensibly simplistic slogans as "violence begets violence," these self-proclaimed pragmatists insist that sometimes massive force is necessary and that in the case of [terrorist leader] Osama bin Laden and [the terrorist group] al-Qaeda little else could possibly serve to diminish the threat of terrorist attack. It takes me back, all this self-assured confidence in the value of preemptive assault. To 1986 in particular, when a co-worker of mine insisted that although our bombing of Libya had failed to kill Colonel [Muammar] Quadafi, that by killing his daughter we had nonetheless served the cause of peace.

Breeding Terrorists

After all, said my co-worker, she was destined to become a terrorist someday, so better to kill her before she grew. That others might be able to apply the same logic to Americans—who, after all could grow up to be Elliot Abrams[2]—was lost on her, as she was convinced the world had been made safer that day.

Of course, come to find out that Libya had not been involved in the terrorist incident for which we claimed to be attacking them, but why bother with details? And of course, just two years after my colleague insisted that our assault on Libya had made us safer, 259 people [killed] in a plane over Lockerbie, Scotland—and eleven more on the ground there—learned how dangerously ignorant such faith really was. They as it turned out became the victims of actual

1. The author refers to Operation Enduring Freedom. The United States believed that the Islamic fundamentalist Taliban regime in Afghanistan harbored terrorists, including al-Qaeda terrorists, thought to be responsible for the terrorist attacks of September 11, 2001. The objective of the operation was to destroy terrorist training camps, capture al-Qaeda leaders, and make clear to Taliban leaders that the harboring of terrorists is unacceptable.   2. Abrams was assistant secretary of state for inter-American affairs during the Ronald Reagan administration. He was responsible for what some consider repressive and illegal policies pursued in El Salvador and Nicaragua during the 1980s. He was convicted of lying to Congress about U.S. affairs in these and other nations.

Libyan terrorists enraged by the previous U.S. attack on their country.

Confusing Naïveté and Realism

All this talk of what's naïve and what is realistic has seemed to be nothing if not bizarre. It's as if words no longer have their original meanings, or perhaps mean the opposite of what one might otherwise think. So to be realistic means to believe that bombing one of the poorest nations on Earth [Afghanistan] will not only reduce terrorism, but also fail to ignite a new round of anti-American fanaticism.

To be naïve, on the other hand, is to pay attention to modern history, which tells us in no uncertain terms that bombing people is rather likely to fuel their anger, resentment, and desire for revenge.

To be realistic is to think that pummeling one nation—in this case Afghanistan—will have some appreciable effect on the thugs in al-Qaeda, despite the fact that the group operates in sixty-four countries including many allies whom we have no intention of bombing.

To be naïve is to point out that terrorists aren't reliant on one, or even several countries to operate, and as such, we could eradicate every member of the Taliban [rulers in Afghanistan] tomorrow without delaying by so much as a day any future attacks on our shores.

To be realistic is to believe our government officials when they insist they have proof of bin Laden's involvement in the [September 11, 2001, terrorist attacks on America]. To be naïve is to wonder how an intelligence community that completely missed the signs of impending disaster, could be so sure, so soon, of who did this thing that they had no idea was coming in the first place. To be really naïve, I guess, would be to think that perhaps they might be lying. Forget that that's exactly what they did so as to justify bombing Quadafi, and what they did when the CIA announced that armed Libyans were roaming the streets of America, planning to assassinate Ronald Reagan.

And it's what they did when they claimed the Soviets were building a military base in Grenada, or that the Sandinistas in Nicaragua were running drugs (actually it was our guys, the contras, who were doing that). And apropos of today's headlines, it's what they did when they decided to dub a certain band of fundamentalist thugs known as the Mujahadeen, "freedom fighters."

Using Force to Bring Justice

To be realistic is to say things like "all they respect is force." To be naïve is to point out that the force we have demonstrated over the years by our support for Israel, or bombing and sanctions against Iraq, has apparently led not to something so kind as their respect for us, but rather to their willingness to slaughter as many Americans as possible. If this is how al-Qaeda shows respect, I shudder to think what disdain must look like.

To be realistic is to say, "we tried peace and peace failed." To be naïve is to ask when, exactly, did the U.S. try peace: in the region, or specifically in Afghanistan? Was it when we were selling Stinger missiles to the Muj, so as to help them fight the Soviets [during the Soviet occupation from 1979 to 1989]?

Or was it after, when we left the nation in ruins, unconcerned about helping rebuild so long as the Russians had fled?

Or was it when we cozied up to the Taliban because they promised to crack down on opium cultivation, using the time-honored anti-crime techniques of extremist Islam?

To be realistic is to insist that nations harboring terrorists must be brought to justice. To be naïve is to note that a) we aren't really serious about that—after all, many nations that do so are coalition partners in the war on Afghanistan; and b) by that standard, any number of nations would have the right to attack us.

After all, we have harbored and even taught terrorists and death squad leaders at the School of the Americas at Fort Benning, Georgia. We have harbored known Cuban terrorists in Miami. We even gave a tax exemption for several years to a neo-Nazi "church" affiliated with the National Alliance, whose leader has called for worldwide racial cleansing, whose words are credited with inspiring [Oklahoma City bomber] Timothy McVeigh, and whose members have committed bombings, murders and armed robberies across the country.

Beneficent Saviors?

To be realistic is to believe that Afghans will be impressed by our packets of peanut butter, dropped from airplanes [as aid during the war], and that they will thank us, and view us as their beneficent saviors.

To be naïve is to point out that the food drops—according to relief agencies—are insufficient to meet the need, especially since our bombing has aggravated the refugee crisis to staggering proportions.

To be really naïve is to note that to even get the food, Afghans would have to traipse across minefields, and that their experience with toy dolls dropped from Soviet planes in the 80's—which turned out to be explosives—might have left them a bit reluctant to tear into our humanitarian goodies.

Playing into Their Hands

The important thing to remember about terrorism is that it is a reflexive phenomenon. Its impact and development depend on the actions and reactions of the victims. If the victims react by turning into perpetrators, terrorism triumphs in the sense of engendering more and more violence. . . . By allowing a "war" on terrorism to become our principal preoccupation, we are playing straight into the terrorists' hands: They—not we—are setting our priorities.

George Soros, *Los Angeles Times*, April 4, 2004.

To be naïve to the point of disloyalty, would, I suppose, be to ask whether or not American soldiers in Pearl Harbor would have felt better about the bombing of December 7, 1941, had the Japanese pilots made a second run to drop sushi and edamame.

To be realistic is to claim that attacks on Afghanistan will lead the pulverized citizenry to overthrow their Taliban oppressors.

To be naïve is to point out that never in history has a nation under attack blamed its own leaders for the attack, but rather, exactly the opposite. After all, in the wake of 9/11,

Americans did not, en masse write to the President demanding he accede to the wishes of Osama bin Laden.

A War on Islam

To be realistic is to insist that this is not a war on Islam.

To be naïve is to point out that if we continue to bomb, especially through the holy month of Ramadan, there will be few Muslims in the world who will believe that. Perhaps it's just me. But something seems dangerously Alice in Wonderland, when [Bill] Clinton Advisor Dick Morris can say on national television that we should declare war on Afghanistan, and then Iraq, Libya, Sudan, and Colombia—and not be viewed as a paragon of mental illness—but Quakers and pacifists are derided as uninformed boobs.

And yet I have no doubt that many of these American warlords will attend Martin Luther King Jr. day celebrations come January [2002], and sing the praises of a man who would have condemned them roundly for their current course of action. And they will continue to go to church—those who call themselves Christians—and sing praises to someone whose teachings run completely counter to everything they are now doing.

But hey—King, [Mohandas] Gandhi, Jesus: what did they know? Dreamers all of them: naïve, simplistic, innocent, and not nearly as informed or clear-headed as say, [Secretary of Defense] Donald Rumsfeld, or [authors] Stephen Ambrose, or Tom Clancy, or White House spokesman Ari Fleischer.

Unusual Suspects

Even more disturbing than the uniformity with which conservatives have labeled dissenters un-American and unrealistic (which at least is to be expected), is the rapidity with which quite a few progressives have accepted the need for, and ultimate propriety of war.

Richard Falk—a longtime international peace expert—has called Operation Enduring Freedom, "the first truly just war since World War II." This, despite the fact that by the standards he himself has laid out for a just war, the bombing of Afghanistan—and the refugee crisis alone that it has sparked—completely fail the test of justice.

Or [journalist] Marc Cooper, who recently suggested that antiwar protesters might suffer from self-hatred, and who accused us of claiming that the U.S. invited the attacks of the 11th, merely because we dare point out the truism that certain of our policies might have something to do with the motivation for flying 757's into buildings. The difference between explanation and excuse apparently having escaped him, and the good counsel of a Thesaurus that might explain the difference apparently being out of his reach, Cooper insists that the left should embrace limited military action (the substance of which he leaves undefined) as a "moral imperative."

And one hardly knows what to make of Eleanor Smeal, of the Fund for the Feminist Majority. She testified to Congress about Afghanistan, not to plead for an end to the macho militarism currently underway, which is likely to accelerate the starvation of perhaps a million women and girls there, but merely to suggest that the women of Afghanistan not be forgotten in any reconstruction government.

Not only does she appear to support the overthrow of the Taliban by the same U.S. government that funded it and cared not a whit for the women there until six weeks ago, but she also seems to trust that patriarchy can be pounded into rubble by exploding phallic symbols, dropped and fired by guys whose view of feminism is probably not much better than Mullah Omar's. Talk about irony.

Again, maybe it's just me. Or maybe it's *1984*, and War Is Peace, and Slavery Is Freedom, and Ignorance Is Strength.[3] Or maybe all that is just bullshit, being served up on a silver platter, while the servers tell us it's really Goose Liver Pate. It reminds me of something my Grandma once said: "You can call your ass a turkey, but that doesn't make it Thanksgiving." Likewise, you can call your war just, and the rest of us naïve, but that won't make it so.

---

3. The author refers to George Orwell's book *1984*, in which language is deliberately crafted to disguise or distort its actual meaning.

Periodical Bibliography

The following articles have been selected to supplement the diverse views presented in this chapter.

Phillip J. Brown	"Justice, Law, and War," *America*, August 18, 2003.
George J. Bryjak	"Don't Call It War—It's Mass Horror," *National Catholic Reporter*, February 7, 2003.
George W. Bush	"Remarks on Iraq," *Representative American Speeches 2002–2003*, 2003.
Jimmy Carter	"Just War—or a Just War?" *New York Times*, March 9, 2003.
Gregory D. Foster	"Just War Doctrine in an Age of Hyperpower Politics," *Humanist*, March/April 2004.
Tom Frame	"Ideology, Morality, and the War in Iraq," *Quadrant*, September 2003.
James Turner Johnson	"Jihad and Just War," *First Things*, June/July 2002.
Marcy Kaptur	"Allies Working Toward a Secure Future," *Representative American Speeches 2002–2003*, 2003.
Michael Kelly	"Is Iraq War Justified?" *Milwaukee Journal Sentinel*, August 16, 2002.
Edward M. Kennedy	"Eliminating the Threat: The Right Course of Action for Disarming Iraq, Combating Terrorism, Protecting the Homeland, and Stabilizing the Middle East," *Representative American Speeches 2002–2003*, 2003.
David R. Loy	"New Holy War Against Evil?" *Conversation*, September 18, 2001.
Rahul Mahajan	"The New Crusade: America's War on Terrorism," *Monthly Review*, February 2002.
Thomas Merton	"The Root of War Is Fear," *National Catholic Reporter*, April 4, 2003.
Ewuare Osayande	"War Is the Enemy of the Poor," *Other Side*, January/February 2003.
Nelofer Pazira	"War and the West's Betrayals," *Maclean's*, November 25, 2002.
Kenneth Roth	"The Law of War in the War on Terror," *Foreign Affairs*, January/February 2004.

Raymond A. Schroth	"Bush Leads 'Peaceful People' to War," *National Catholic Reporter*, March 28, 2003.
Jim Wallis	"War Lessons Learned," *New Catholic Times*, April 20, 2003.
Howard Zinn	"A Just Cause, Not a Just War," *Progressive*, December 2001.

CHAPTER 3

How Should War Be Conducted?

Chapter Preface

In early May 2004, a little over a year after a U.S.-led coalition ousted Iraqi dictator Saddam Hussein, videos and photographs of U.S. soldiers abusing Iraqi prisoners held at Abu Ghraib prison in Iraq flooded the media. The images generated shock and outrage around the globe and prompted debates about America's use of torture during its war on terrorism.

International law regarding the abuse of prisoners is clear. The "use of force, mental torture, threats, insults and exposure to unpleasant and inhumane treatment of any kind" is expressly prohibited by the Geneva Conventions, a series of international agreements that establish rules for the conduct of war, including the treatment of prisoners of war (POWs). Anthony Dworkin, editor of the Crimes of War Project, explains,

> The Geneva Conventions were drafted in the aftermath of World War II, when public anger at the treatment of POWs and captured civilians by the Axis powers [Germany, Italy, and Japan] was running high. They set a high standard for the treatment of all detainees and appear to allow little scope for the forceful interrogation of captives. These standards are absolute—there is no scope for them to be altered in the face of terrorism or insurgency.

Since the terrorist attacks of September 11, 2001, however, some analysts have begun to discuss whether the use of torture is justified in the face of imminent national security threats. According to Charles B. Strozier, director of the Center on Terrorism at John Jay College of the City University of New York, "Nobody defended torture before 9-11. . . . Now people suddenly embrace torture big time." However, after the release of the photographs from Abu Ghraib, the implications of these calls for torture became painfully clear. Claims Douglas A. Johnson, executive director of the Center for Victims of Torture, "It's not an abstract thing anymore. . . . It really personalizes the issue. The glee in our soldiers' faces is so incongruous with our values."

Some commentators fear that the failure to observe the rules of the Geneva Conventions prohibiting torture threatens America's reputation as a representative of freedom and democracy. Michael Ignatieff, director of the Carr Center of

Human Rights Policy at Harvard University, argues, "Liberal democracy stands against torture because it stands against any unlimited use of public authority against human beings, and torture is the most unlimited, the most unbridled form of power that one person can exercise against another."

Still other observers express concern that the torture of prisoners in violation of the Geneva Conventions jeopardizes U.S. credibility. After all, they point out, one objection to Hussein's regime was its torturing of Iraqi citizens. In fact, after Hussein's capture on December 24, 2003, President George W. Bush said, "For the vast majority of Iraqi citizens who wish to live as free men and women, this event brings further assurance that the torture chambers and the secret police are gone forever." The revelation of the abuse of Iraqi prisoners at Abu Ghraib challenges the credibility of such statements, many critics contend. Senator Robert Byrd asks, "Given the catastrophic impact that this scandal has had on the world community, how can the United States ever repair its credibility? How are we supposed to convince not only the Iraqi people but also the rest of the world that America is, indeed, a liberator and not a conqueror, not an arrogant power?" Senator Edward M. Kennedy adds, "Shamefully, we now learn that Saddam's torture chambers reopened under new management—U.S. management."

Joseph Loconte, a scholar at the conservative Heritage Foundation, disagrees with these assessments. Loconte argues that comparing the abuse at Abu Ghraib to the horrors conducted by dictators such as Hussein is unfair: "American democracy owes much of its success to its commitment to the rule of law—a rule that was shattered at Abu Ghraib. Yet it is a moral perversion to blur the distinction between America's imperfect democracy and genocidal dictatorships. That tactic . . . will further weaken America's standing and influence in the world."

The full impact of the abuse of Iraqi prisoners at Abu Ghraib remains to be seen. The authors in the following chapter debate similar issues concerning *jus in bello*—the laws governing the conduct of war.

"Combatants captured during an international armed conflict should be presumed to be POWs."

Detainees in the War on Terror Should Be Treated as Prisoners of War

Bruce Shapiro

The United States should respect the rules of conducting war established by the Geneva Conventions and treat those detained in the war on terror as prisoners of war, argues Bruce Shapiro in the following viewpoint. Labeling detainees "unlawful combatants" and thus exempting itself from the rules of war may help the United States gain more information during interrogation, Shapiro claims. However, if the United States expects its soldiers to be treated according to the rules, it should not undermine these rules to achieve its own short-term objectives. Shapiro is a contributing editor for *Nation* and Salon.com.

As you read, consider the following questions:
1. According to Shapiro, what memories were conjured by the images of Afghan prisoners shipped hooded, shackled, and sedated to an unknown location?
2. In the author's view, what does the shock expressed by U.S. allies at the method of transport and incarceration at Guantánamo show?
3. With what have Donald Rumsfeld and George W. Bush replaced evolving international law?

Bruce Shapiro, "POWs in Legal Limbo," *The Nation*, February 25, 2002.

It's safe to assume that the 150 or so Al Qaeda and Taliban militiamen[1] now occupying those 6-by-8-foot cages in Guantánamo Bay [Cuba] are not sympathetic characters. It's also reasonable, and important, to say that they are in less danger to life and limb than their comrades handed over by the United States to the Northern Alliance [an Afghan movement opposed to the ousted Taliban regime]. While the Western press has focused almost exclusively on Camp X-Ray [a Guantánamo Bay prison], Amnesty International reported on February 1 [2002] that "the lives of thousands of prisoners in Afghanistan are at risk" from hunger and "rampant" dysentery, pneumonia and hepatitis, in overcrowded prison camps where inmates suffer shortages of food and medical supplies and "are not sheltered from severe winter conditions."

Shocking the World

The fact that Camp X-Ray comes out ahead of the dreadful prevailing POW standard in postwar Afghanistan does the United States no credit. The image of prisoners shipped hooded, shackled and sedated to an unknown location was a foreign-policy disaster: in Europe, the Mideast and Asia alike, conjuring raw memories of the most vicious hostage-takings. Defense Secretary [Donald] Rumsfeld's insistence that X-Ray's prisoners fall outside the protections of the Geneva Conventions and the US Constitution only furthered the impression of an Administration descending to the brutal law-enforcement benchmark of an authoritarian regime like Saudi Arabia. (Evidently the Administration just wants its guests to feel at home: Saudis count for at least 100 of the Guantánamo prisoners.) The White House's February 7 [2002] turnabout, declaring that Geneva Convention rules apply to Taliban captives but not Al Qaeda [terrorists in Guantánamo Bay], amounts to a fig leaf satisfying neither the specific requirements of the accords nor the broader sense of alarm worldwide.

---

1. Al Qaeda, a terrorist group established by Saudi millionaire Osama bin Laden in the late 1980s, is composed of Islamic extremists who oppose Western ideals. Taliban militiamen, also a group of Islamic extremists who oppose Western ideals, are young men who came from the poverty-stricken Afghan refugee camps during the Soviet-Afghan war.

In part the shock expressed by US allies at the method of transport and incarceration at Guantánamo shows the huge gap between Europe and the United States on prisons and punishment. Western European prisons, for the most part, come nowhere near the degrading and isolating inmate-control regimens in many US facilities. Camp X-Ray is a close cousin to supermax penitentiaries with their psychically debilitating twenty-three-hour-a-day solitary confinement and twenty-four-hour cell lighting.

An Inaccurate Label

But comparing X-Ray to conventional prisons, and Afghanistan militia to conventional prisoners, only forces the questions Rumsfeld and the White House have tried so hard to obfuscate: Are the prisoners POWs or criminals? Just what rights should these international brigades of clerical fascism retain, as the losing side in a war backed by the United States but fought largely by proxy forces? Rumsfeld and the White House insist that neither Taliban nor Al Qaeda are prisoners of war but instead "unlawful combatants," suggesting that they don't deserve the numerous protections afforded POWs, most famously the right to respond to questions with name, rank and serial number but also including rights to representation, repatriation and due process. The Administration is now willing to admit that Taliban militia, as the former army of Afghanistan, are at least covered by the accords' broader humanitarian provisions; but the majority of Guantánamo prisoners—those Al Qaeda "Arab Afghans" who fought as allies of the Taliban regime—the White House still casts completely outside the protection of the Geneva Conventions.

A press outspun by Rumsfeld's daily patter has missed the simple fact that, as law, this argument has more holes than a Tora Bora cave [where Al Qaeda terrorists hid in Afghanistan] after US bombardment. "Unlawful combatants" is a phrase found nowhere in the Geneva accords. Here is how Human Rights Watch summarizes it: "Under international humanitarian law, combatants captured during an international armed conflict should be presumed to be POWs until determined otherwise." Only a court or other "competent tribunal"—not the Defense Secretary or the President—can make that determination. In fact, the Pentagon's own Judge Advocate General Handbook declares that "when doubt exists" about a prisoner's status, "tribunals must be convened"—as they were for Iraqi prisoners in the Gulf War.

Rall. © 2002 by Universal Press Syndicate. Reproduced by permission.

The United States has good reason to care about these procedures. During the Vietnam War, Hanoi declared captured US fliers "unlawful combatants." It was Washington that insisted otherwise; in 1977 the United States made sure that the Geneva protocols were revised to insure that anyone captured in war is protected by the treaty whether civilian, military or in between, whether or not they technically meet the POW definition. Simply put, when President [George W.] Bush unilaterally declares the majority of its prisoners outside the penumbra of the Geneva Convention, he is still flouting both international law and international sensibility.

A Troubling New Attitude

The trouble with placing Guantánamo's prisoners in a legal no man's land doesn't end there. If captured militia are not

POWs then they can continue to be held only if they're individually charged with war crimes or other specific offenses. If that should happen to the Guantánamo prisoners, they're entitled to a "fair and regular trial" (a standard that almost certainly cannot be met by the drumhead courts authorized by Bush).

Bush's latest policy turn amounts to internment without trial for alleged Al Qaeda. It's entirely appropriate to want to question the Al Qaeda mafia's foot soldiers, and there are plenty of legitimate claims on the prosecution of Al Qaeda, from citizens in Kabul [Afghanistan] and New York and points between. But the way to go about both is through existing criminal and international laws—an approach that gets results, as the victims of [Chilean war criminal] Gen. Augusto Pinochet proved in courts on two continents. The Rumsfeld-Bush strategy, on the other hand, undermines the idea of cooperative transnational prosecution and representation of victims, replacing evolving international law with an autocratic extension of this Administration's foreign-policy unilateralism: If we can live without the ABM treaty, why not pitch those troublesome Geneva accords over the side as well?

The Risk of a Backfire

In the Administration only [U.S. Secretary of State] Colin Powell understands how profoundly this shortsighted approach runs counter to the national interest. Powell is no friend of human rights. But he pushed so hard—winning the compromise of Geneva Convention recongition for Taliban prisoners—because as a former military man he knows that the United States, the world's number-one projector of force, has its own reasons to seek universal respect for the Geneva Conventions—conventions we instantly invoked when American pilots were shot down in the Persian Gulf, and again in the Balkans. Powell knows, too, that the whole logic of the Geneva accords—those special POW protections—is to entice losing combatants into pragmatic and dignified surrender. By making a transnational mockery of the Geneva protocols, Rumsfeid and Bush are inviting future enemies to conclude that suicidal escalation, rather than surrender, is the only sensible closing chapter of their *jihad* [an Islamic holy war].

Rumsfeld is hell-bent on turning the prisoners of Camp X-Ray into legal nonpersons—essentially stateless, without the safe harbor of either international law or the US Constitution, granted status and rights only at the whim of the Defense Secretary. That may seem to serve the short-term goals of Al Qaeda interrogation, but the picture it presents to the world—a superpower playing semantic games with the most basic wartime covenants, setting back the evolving machinery for transnational justice—will generate its own unhappy blowback.

"*Whatever one thinks of the way we treat detainees . . . one cannot argue that they are POWs under international or American law.*"

Detainees in the War on Terror Should Not Be Treated as Prisoners of War

Ronald D. Rotunda

According to Ronald D. Rotunda in the following viewpoint, American and international law hold that the detainees in the war on terror should not be considered prisoners of war. Detainees should not be treated as POWs, he claims, because they do not meet the preconditions set by the Geneva Conventions, which codified when and how war is to be conducted. Rotunda maintains, for example, that al Qaeda terrorists do not wear uniforms or openly carry arms, prerequisites for being considered POWs. Rotunda is a professor at the University of Illinois College of Law.

As you read, consider the following questions:

1. In Rotunda's opinion, how does American constitutional law support the assertion that detainees in the war on terror are not POWs?
2. In the author's view, why does the Geneva Convention require soldiers to wear fixed, distinctive emblems visible from afar?
3. How does Rotunda answer those who claim it is crucial to the status of detainees that the United States has not "declared war"?

Ronald D. Rotunda, "No POWs," www.nationalreview.com, January 29, 2002. Copyright © 2002 by National Review, Inc., 215 Lexington Ave., New York, NY 10016. Reproduced by permission of United Feature Syndicate, Inc.

The United States says that the [Taliban and terrorist group al Qaeda] prisoners held in [Guantánamo Bay] Cuba are "unlawful combatants," not prisoners of war. Some critics treat this as all word play. There is a war, they became prisoners, and that makes them POWs, right? Wrong. Whatever one thinks of the way we treat detainees (the news has reported that some have no complaints while others repeatedly threaten to kill their guards), one cannot argue that they are POWs under international or American law.

Examining Constitutional Law

First, let's turn to American constitutional law. In *Ex Parte Quirin* (1942), the Supreme Court upheld the jurisdiction of a military commission that convicted German saboteurs who landed in the United States to commit acts of war. The Germans trained them in the use of explosives and other sabotage techniques. They buried their German Marine Infantry uniforms immediately upon landing. The Supreme Court said that the soldiers thereby became "unlawful combatants . . . subject to trial and punishment by military commission for acts which render their belligerency unlawful."

Seven of the eight soldiers were born in Germany while one was a United States citizen. All eight, who had lived in the United States, returned to Germany between 1933 and 1941. The United States did not treat the saboteurs as POWs. Instead, it treated them as "unlawful combatants," tried them by military tribunal, and executed most of them.

The end of World War II saw more military tribunals. There was, of course, the multinational Nuremberg warcrimes tribunal, but there were many more national warcrimes tribunals. Nuremberg handled about 200 cases but the United States Army Judge Advocate prosecuted another 1,600 war-crimes defendants. French and British tribunals had their own military tribunals.

The Geneva Convention

Now, let's turn to international law. Both Afghanistan and the United States ratified the third Geneva Convention of 1949, which sets out basic protections for POWs, but they must be "lawful combatants" for the treaty to apply.

The Geneva Convention sets out four key preconditions. First, the soldiers must be part of an organized command structure, so that leaders can be held responsible. Second, the soldiers must wear fixed distinctive emblems visible from afar—so that the other side can avoid killing civilians without fearing attack from disguised fighters. Third, the soldiers must carry arms openly. Fourth, the other side must show respect for the laws of war, for example, by not taking hostages.

The Geneva Convention Does Not Apply to Terrorists

Terrorists are not soldiers. They have no rank and they have no uniform. In fact, al Qaeda goes out of its way to operate in independent cells with no command structure. Terrorists do not fight in battlefields, and they do not fight under the authority of governments. Most importantly, their targets are almost always innocent civilians. These are not soldiers, and as such the prisoner of war provisions of the Geneva Convention do not apply to them.

Joe Pitts, U.S. House of Representatives Commentary, January 29, 2002.

Al Qaeda repeatedly violated these preconditions before, after, and during the Sept. 11 [2001, terrorist] attacks. The al Qaeda terrorists target civilians; they do not wear uniforms; they do not carry arms openly; they take hostages (such as the hostages they took when they hijacked the four airplanes on Sept. 11). The Taliban leadership [in Afghanistan] harbored, aided, and abetted [al Qaeda leader] Osama bin Laden and al Qaeda in their violations of the laws of war, and al Qaeda, in return, financed the Taliban. The Taliban soldiers, or many of them, committed war crimes, such as hiding weapons in mosques, and using their own people as human shields.

The Geneva Protocol allows non-state belligerents to secure protected treatment under the protocol. They just have to file a declaration with the Swiss government accepting the obligations of the protocol. When al Qaeda does that, then it will receive the benefits of POW status.

Some people argue that we should treat war criminals as POWs so that terrorists will be nicer to our citizens. Or will al Qaeda see this as more weakness by a paper tiger? Does al

Qaeda respect strength or weakness? However you answer these questions, realize that if we treat the Cuban prisoners as POWs we will be giving them something to which they are not entitled under international or American law.

War Need Not Be Declared

Of course, whether or not we treat the detainees as POWs, they should have trials and these trials should be fair. If the government cannot prove that a defendant has violated the Geneva Convention or the laws of war, he should be set free. In deciding these issues, there are those who say that it is crucial that the United States has not "declared" war. Not so.

The Constitution gives to Congress the sole power to "declare" war. The Founders specifically rejected a proposal that only Congress could "make war." The last declared war that the U.S. fought was WWII. The Korean War, the Vietnam War, etc., were never declared. The Civil War, the bloodiest war in U.S. history, was never declared.

The framers—and international law at the time—understood that one does not need to "declare" war in order to fight in a war of self-defense. Only aggressive war need be declared, and the U.N. treaty outlaws that. Under the historical view of the war power, there was no need to declare WWII (although we did so). Nor was there any need to declare the Gulf War, because a state, like Kuwait, always has the right of self-defense, and it can ask other states for assistance. Under the U.N. Charter, we could assist Kuwait because we had no intention of waging an aggressive war. And under the U.N. Charter we also have the right to defend ourselves when subjected to acts of war, like the attacks of September 11th.

"Combatant nations are not allowed to slaughter civilians in order to spare combatants."

Civilians Should Not Be Targeted to Spare Combatants

Brian Carnell

In the following viewpoint Brian Carnell argues that when nations target civilians to reduce their military's casualties, they are acting immorally and against international rules of war. According to Carnell, those who claim that targeting civilians is sometimes necessary to win wars often mistakenly cite the bombing of Hiroshima, Japan, and Dresden, Germany, cities that were in fact targeted after Allied forces were assured of victory in World War II. Targeting civilians is the method of choice of terrorists, claims Carnell, and killing civilians often stiffens their resolve to resist the occupying force. Carnell, a video conferencing manager, maintains a weblog at http://Brian.Carnell.com.

As you read, consider the following questions:

1. In Carnell's view, how is collateral damage distinguished from the deliberate targeting of civilians?
2. What was at issue when U.S. president Harry S. Truman decided to bomb Hiroshima and then Nagasaki, in the author's opinion?
3. According to Andrew Dalton, why was the United States not as lucky in Vietnam as it was against the Taliban?

Fredrik Norman [a Libertarian writer] points to this rant by Andrew Dalton [an Objectivist writer] about whether or not it is ever appropriate during a war to *intentionally* target civilians. The short version is that most Libertarians say that it is never appropriate, while some Objectivists assert that it is:

The Objectivist View

Dalton writes, [in] *Libertarian Watch:*

> The one thing that seems to unite all libertarians—other than their nominal support of "liberty"—is their disdain for Objectivism. For instance, Charles Oliver writes,
>
>> Most people accept that some civilian casualties are inevitable in war, and the fact that civilians might die isn't necessarily a good reason to forego any particular military action. Does this mean that we can, as the Ayn Rand Institute folks urge, deliberately target civilians?
>
> He continues on with usual "No, that would make us terrorists too" arguments. But he leaves out two important contexts. The first is that deliberately targeting civilians (as opposed to killing civilians incidentally during an attack on a military or industrial target) is an extreme act that would not be justified in most military actions. It was justified during World War II, when our enemies had both the will and the means to destroy us utterly. Oliver takes issue with the mass destruction of Dresden [Germany] and Hiroshima [Japan], but would he even be alive today to complain if the Allies had not destroyed those cities?

Note that what we are not talking about here is collateral damage. Everyone who accepts some sort of just war theory acknowledges that civilians are going to be killed inadvertently in war. But the issue before us is whether or not there is any situation in which it would be okay to say, "There are some noncombatant civilians over there—lets bomb them to get this war over with."

Examining Objectivist Reasoning

Dalton cites two examples where civilians were intentionally bombed by Allied forces during World War II—Dresden and Hiroshima—and implies that some of us might not even be alive if it weren't for these two bombings. Dalton needs to check his premises.

Both Dresden and Hiroshima were bombed when the ultimate outcome of the war was clear.

Dresden was firebombed on Feb. 13–14, 1945 and estimates put the number of dead civilians at 35,000–150,000. Ironically, many of those killed in Dresden were refugees who were fleeing the advance of the Soviet Army into Germany.

Turning Soldiers into Terrorists

One could formulate a cold-blooded moral equation along the following lines: Targeting civilians is an appropriate strategy whenever the justice of the cause multiplied by the likelihood of success exceeds the human cost, if we measure "justice of the cause" by the number of lives to be saved . . . ; "likelihood of success" by the mathematical probability that the killing will in fact help the cause; and "human cost" by the number of civilians to be killed.

Does this mean that sometimes targeting civilians is OK? Absolutely not, contends professor Philip Bobbitt of the University of Texas Law School, the author of . . . *The Shield of Achilles*, [which] explores deeply the history of war and law: "The terrorist does not reluctantly accept the accidental killings that accompany warfare; his whole point is to kill ordinary people in order to make them fearful. If we make targeting civilians lawful, we turn our armed forces into terrorists."

Stuart Taylor, *Atlantic Monthly*, April 16, 2002.

There have been a number of efforts to offer military purposes behind the bombing of Dresden, but the decision to bomb the city seems to have been heavily influenced by Bomber Command head Arthur Harris who was an advocate of the use of area bombing of civilian areas to demoralize the population and hasten a surrender.

Hiroshima, of course, was nuked on August 6, 1945. U.S. President Harry Truman made the decision to bomb Hiroshima and then Nagasaki based largely on estimates that an invasion of Japan by Allied forces would result in enormous Allied casualties.

The issue at Hiroshima was not the survival of the free, democratic West, but rather how the occupation of Japan could be accomplished with a minimum number of casualties to Allied military forces.

Applying Just War Theory

The problem is that in most just war theories, combatant nations are not allowed to slaughter civilians in order to spare combatants. The claim that combatants should be allowed to target civilians is at the heart of the argument for terrorism.

Among those justifying Palestinian suicide bombers who target Israeli civilians, for example, a common refrain is that given the might of the Israeli military, the Palestinians have no choice but to target Israeli civilians.

For Dalton, on the other hand, if anything the U.S. government does not target civilians *enough:*

> Now with the way that the war had been fought up to that point, there was no good reason to believe that the Taliban [in Afghanistan] would fall so easily [in 2001]. In simple terms, we got lucky. We didn't get lucky in Vietnam. The fact is, our government was too concerned with civilian casualties (and the worthless opinions of our Arab "allies") to fight the war in a manner that would ensure a certain victory. And the jury is still out on what kind of victory we got.

Of course the Vietnam example shows the flip side of the argument against targeting casualties. Civilian casualties—especially those inflicted by the series of corrupt South Vietnamese governments supported by the United States—seriously undermined support for the U.S. within Vietnam. In fact, if anything intentionally targeting civilians does not seem to demoralize a civilian population and hasten an end to a war as much as it seems to stiffen the resolve and support of civilians for even the most wretched of governments.

It is difficult to argue that civilians should *never* be targeted—in fact nuclear deterrence relies on just such a targeting and I think that can be defended on grounds of efficacy and proportionality. But I've never seen a convincing argument that the attacks on Dresden, Hiroshima or Nagasaki were morally just.

> "*Victory with a minimum of one's own casualties may even require a free nation to deliberately target the civilians of an aggressor.*"

Civilians Should Sometimes Be Targeted to Spare Combatants

Onkar Ghate

Free nations such as the United States have the responsibility to act in self-defense on behalf of their citizens and defeat enemies that attack them, claims Onkar Ghate in the following viewpoint. To defeat aggressors, free nations may have to target civilians in the aggressor nation if the enemy is hiding its soldiers amongst them, Ghate maintains. Moreover, civilians that support governments that attack free nations are not innocent, he claims. Ghate is a senior fellow at the Ayn Rand Institute, an organization that advocates capitalism and the pursuit of individual freedom.

As you read, consider the following questions:
1. According to Ghate, what is the fundamental responsibility of the government of free nations?
2. What moral principles does the author cite in support of the bombings of Dresden, Hamburg, Hiroshima, and Nagasaki at the end of World War II?
3. In the author's opinion, who are the first innocent victims of terrorist governments?

Amid calls from Afghani leaders to stop our bombings [in 2001] in order to prevent further civilian casualties and debates about how to take the war on terrorism elsewhere, one legitimately wonders whether the war will be a success. The efficiency and bravery of our military is cause for optimism. The administration's fear of killing civilians in enemy territory, which first enabled Taliban soldiers and leaders to take shelter in populated areas and later to escape capture, is worrying.

If our war on terrorism is to have any chance of success in such places as Iraq, which is more heavily populated and industrialized than Afghanistan, we must recognize that our government's concern—shared by many Americans—about killing civilians is morally mistaken.

The Role of Government

The government of a free nation is simply the agent of its citizens, charged with one fundamental responsibility: to secure the individual rights—and very lives—of its citizens through the use of retaliatory force. An aspect of this responsibility is to uphold each citizen's right to self-defense, a responsibility our government in part meets by eliminating terrorist states that threaten U.S. citizens.

If, however, in waging war our government considers the deaths of civilians in terrorist states as a cost that must be weighed against the deaths of our own soldiers or civilians, or as a cost that must be weighed against achieving victory over the enemy, our government thereby violates its most basic function. It becomes not an agent for our self-defense, but theirs.

Morally, the U.S. government must destroy our aggressors by whatever means are necessary and minimize U.S. casualties in the process.

To be victorious in war, a free nation has to destroy enough of the aggressor to break his will to continue attacking (and, then, dismantle his war apparatus and replace his government). In modern warfare, this almost always necessitates "collateral damage," i.e., the killing of civilians.

In fact, victory with a minimum of one's own casualties may even require a free nation to deliberately target the

133

civilians of an aggressor nation in order to cripple its economic production and/or break its will. This is what the United States did in WWII when it dropped fire bombs on Dresden and Hamburg [in Germany] and atomic bombs on Hiroshima and Nagasaki [in Japan]. These bombings were moral acts. The destruction of Hiroshima and Nagasaki, for instance, precipitated Japan's surrender and so achieved victory with no further U.S. casualties. In that context, to sacrifice the lives of hundreds of thousands of U.S. soldiers in a ground attack on Japan would have been morally monstrous.

Answering Objections

But, it will be objected, is it not more monstrous to kill all those innocent civilians?

No. The moral principle is: the responsibility for all deaths in war lies with the aggressor who initiates force, not with those who defend themselves.

Further, the objection contains a mistaken assumption: it is false that every civilian in enemy territory—whether we are speaking of Hitler's Germany or Hirohito's Japan or the Taliban's Afghanistan or [Saddam] Hussein's Iraq—is innocent.

The Consequences of Aggression

To the extent that the aggressor is responsible for the consequences of his actions and all justified responses to those actions, he is also responsible for the lives of those people he holds hostage in the war. This is true even when the conflict comes to the aggressor's home. The aggressor may not find moral immunity by hiding his military in civilian centers. To the extent that an aggressor hides the guilty among the innocent, and to the extent that an aggressor exploits civilians in the pursuit of his aggression, innocent and harmless civilians become threats to the retaliating force. They may be innocent, but they have been placed at risk by the aggressor's actions—not by the nation attempting to retaliate.

Patrick Stephens, *Navigator*, November 2001.

Many civilians in the Mid-East, for example, hate us and actively support, materially and/or spiritually, those plotting our deaths. Can one seriously maintain, for instance, that the individuals in the Mid-East who celebrated by dancing in the streets [after the terrorist attacks] on September 11 [2001] are innocent?

Other civilians in enemy states are passive, unthinking followers. Their work and economic production, however meager, supports their terrorist governments and so they are in part responsible for the continued power of our enemies. They too are not innocent—and their deaths may be unavoidable in order for America to defend itself. (Remember too that today's civilian is tomorrow's soldier.)

But what of those who truly are innocent?

The civilians in enemy territory who actually oppose their dictatorial, terrorist governments are usually their governments' first innocent victims. Any such individuals who remain alive and outside of prison camps should try to flee their country or fight with us (as some did in Afghanistan).

And the truly innocent who live in countries that initiate force against other nations will acknowledge the moral right of a free nation to bomb their countries and destroy their governments—even if this jeopardizes their own lives. No truly innocent civilian in Nazi Germany, for example, would have questioned the morality of the Allies razing Germany, even if he knew he may die in the attacks. No truly innocent individual wishes to become a tool of or a shield for his murderous government; he wishes to see his government toppled.

We should not allow human shields, innocent or otherwise, to deter us from defending ourselves.

The U.S. government recognized the truth of this on September 11 [2001] when, in order to defend those citizens it could, it ordered the shooting down of any more airplanes-become-missiles, even though this meant killing not only the terrorists but also the innocent American civilians captive onboard.

The government must now recognize that the same principle applies to civilian casualties in the Mid-East.

War is terrible but sometimes necessary. To win the war on terrorism, we must not let a mistaken concern with "innocents" deter us. As a free nation, we have the moral right to defend ourselves, even if this requires mass civilian deaths in terrorist countries.

> "The United States [should] uphold the
> strict standards of international
> humanitarian law."

The United States Should Uphold Strict International Laws of War

Michael Byers

The United States has the responsibility to uphold strict international laws of war, asserts Michael Byers in the following viewpoint. The laws of war were created to balance military necessity and humanitarian concerns, Byers claims; thus U.S. military strategies that target civilians and employ inhumane weapons to further political and economic rather than military goals violate the spirit of these laws. If the United States expects other nations to honor humanitarian laws of war, it must also respect them. Byers, professor of law at Duke University, is author of *The Rule of Law in International Politics*.

As you read, consider the following questions:
1. In Byers's opinion, why were the obligations to prohibit the direct targeting of civilians taken seriously during Desert Storm?
2. In the author's view, what are the five strategic rings of a regime?
3. According to the author, why should belligerents use the most accurate weapons available to them?

Michael Byers, "The Laws of War, U.S.-Style," *London Review of Books*, vol. 25, February 20, 2003. Appears here by permission of the *London Review of Books*.

More than three hundred Iraqi civilians died on 13 February 1991 when two US F-117 stealth bombers targeted the al-Amiriya bunker in Baghdad [during the Gulf War]. Photographs of the charred and twisted bodies of women and children shocked a world which . . . had seen little of the horrors of the Gulf War. Pentagon officials, who claimed to have intelligence indicating the bunker was a command and control centre, denied knowledge of the civilian presence. Had they known, the attack would probably have been classed as a war crime.

The Humanitarian Laws of War

International humanitarian law, the *jus in bello*, concerns the way wars may be fought. It is distinct from the law governing when wars may be fought (the *jus ad bellum* of self-defence and the UN [United Nations] Charter). Also known as the 'laws of war', international humanitarian law traces its origins to 1859, when the Swiss businessman Henri Dunant witnessed the aftermath of the Battle of Solferino and initiated a movement that became the International Committee of the Red Cross [ICRC]. Today, the rules of international humanitarian law are found in the 1907 Hague Conventions, the 1949 Geneva Conventions and their two Additional Protocols of 1977, as well as in a parallel body of unwritten customary international law that binds all countries, including those that have not ratified the Conventions and Protocols. A central principle prohibits the direct targeting of civilians, as well as attacks on military targets that could be expected to cause civilian suffering disproportionate to the specific military goals to be achieved.

During the first Gulf War, these obligations were taken seriously. Desert Storm was the first major combat operation undertaken by the United States since the Vietnam War. Fearful of another domestic backlash if things went wrong, the politicians left the conduct of hostilities to professional soldiers—who are trained to fight by the book. Adherence to the rule of law was further aided by the 18-member coalition. Some US allies accord considerable importance to the requirements of international humanitarian law, and so, in order to maintain the coalition, the US had to fight according to the rules.

Some two hundred military lawyers were dispatched to the Gulf. They vetted every target: a strike on a statue of Saddam Hussein in Baghdad was ruled out because only targets that contributed to the Iraqi war effort were permissible under international humanitarian law. Those legal controversies that arose stemmed from differing interpretations of the law, rather than any desire to ignore legal constraints. For example, when the US used cluster bombs and fuel-air explosives to attack Iraqi armour, at least five British officers resigned their commissions having seen the effects these weapons had on Iraqi soldiers. A similar divergence of views arose over the use of earthmovers and tank-mounted ploughs to bury Iraqi soldiers alive in their trenches, thus avoiding the dangers of hand-to-hand combat. International humanitarian law forbids methods of warfare that cause 'unnecessary suffering or superfluous injury', but what do these terms actually mean? Wars are fought to be won; international humanitarian law merely balances military necessity against humanitarian concerns. Where one sets the balance depends on where one's coming from: the insular, individualistic, religious character of the US would seem to matter here.

A Change in American Attitudes

After decades of massive defence spending, the US is today assured of victory in any war it chooses to fight. High-tech weaponry has reduced the dangers to US personnel, making it easier to sell war to domestic constituencies. As a result, some US politicians have begun to think of war, not as the high-risk recourse of last resort, but as an attractive foreign policy option in times of domestic scandal or economic decline. This change in thinking has already led to a more cavalier approach to the *jus ad bellum*, as exemplified by the Bush doctrine of pre-emptive self-defence. It is beginning to have a similar effect with regard to the *jus in bello*. When war is seen as an ordinary tool of foreign policy—'politics by other means'—political and financial considerations impinge on the balance between military necessity and humanitarian concerns. Soldiers are buried alive because the folks back home don't like body bags.

In Washington, it has become accepted wisdom that future opponents are themselves unlikely to abide by international humanitarian law. During the Gulf War, captured American pilots were brutalised in several ways—some, for example, were gang-raped. The September 2001 attacks on the Twin Towers were 'crimes against humanity'—in technical terms, they were acts of violence committed as part of a systematic attack on a civilian population. If your enemy is going to cheat, why bother playing by the rules?

The Advice of Civilian Lawyers

[Secretary of Defense] Donald Rumsfeld's own disdain for international humanitarian law was apparent in January 2002, when suspected Taliban and al-Qaida[1] members were transported to the US naval base in Guantanamo Bay. Ignoring criticism from a number of European leaders, the UN High Commissioner for Human Rights and even the normally neutral Red Cross, Rumsfeld insisted the detainees were not prisoners of war and refused to convene the tribunals required under the Geneva Conventions to determine their status. He also ignored advice from the Pentagon's judge advocate generals, and based his decision instead on an analysis provided by White House counsel Alberto Gonzales, a former corporate lawyer from Texas. The suspects, who have still not been charged or granted access to counsel, remain at Guantanamo: at least 14 have attempted suicide.

There is no love lost between the Defense Secretary and his military lawyers. In October 2002, CIA operatives used a Predator drone to track the Taliban leader Mullah Omar to a building in a residential area of Kabul. An air strike was called off because a lawyer at US Central Command was concerned about the risk of disproportionate civilian casualties. According to a report in the *New Yorker*, the incident left Rumsfeld 'kicking a lot of glass and breaking doors'. The Secretary has subsequently taken steps to reduce the number of lawyers in uniform.

1. The Taliban is a fundamentalist Islamic regime that ruled Afghanistan until it was toppled in the US-led war against terror in Afghanistan in 2001. Al-Qaida, a terrorist group established by Saudi millionaire Osama bin Laden in the late 1980s, is composed of Islamic extremists who oppose Western ideals.

The Targeting of Civilians

Rumsfeld has also been encouraging a re-evaluation of the prohibition on targeting civilians, particularly with regard to actions directed at shattering support for the opponent regime. This kind of thinking was popular during the Second World War—as evidenced by the firebombing of Dresden and Hamburg [Germany]—but was subsequently rejected during the negotiation of the Geneva Conventions. Today, a theory which holds that a regime has 'five strategic rings' is attracting adherents in Washington. According to this view, each ring represents a different facet of a society: its political leadership, economic system, supporting infrastructure, population and military forces. Air power is supposed to enable the United States to target opponents from the 'inside out', to bypass military forces and go directly for the political leadership. In this context, the indirect targeting of civilians—through the destruction of bridges, electrical grids, oil refineries and water-filtration plants—is considered justified because it hastens the course of the conflict (while, incidentally, reducing the cost of victory).

During the first Gulf War, the US targeted the Iraqi national grid, shutting down hospitals as well as water and sewage pumping stations. The health consequences for civilians were severe, but the strikes were legal even so: Iraqi military communications depended heavily on the grid. In 1999, when [Yugoslavian President] Slobodan Milosevic's forces proved considerably more resilient than expected, the US pushed for the adoption of a looser approach. Electrical grids and water-filtration plants in Serbia were targeted, not in order to disrupt the actions of the Yugoslav Army in Kosovo, but in an effort to provoke domestic opposition to the regime in Belgrade.

In 1991, a number of coalition planes (RAF Tornados especially) were lost to Iraqi anti-aircraft fire because they were bombing from low altitudes in order to reduce civilian casualties. Less accurate high-altitude strikes by B-52s were restricted to targets well clear of civilian areas. In the Kosovo conflict, almost all the bombing was carried out beyond the reach of Serbian air defences. As a result NATO [North Atlantic Treaty Organization] pilots were sometimes unable to distinguish between military and civilian targets. Again, as a result of US pressure there is now a different reckoning of the balance between military necessity and humanitarian concerns.

Avoiding Higher Standards

The Kosovo conflict was complicated by the fact that Yugoslavia had ratified Additional Protocol One, which imposes stricter protections for civilians. Since every member of NATO apart from the US had also ratified the protocol, certain types of mission were allocated only to US pilots. Canadian pilots, who train with their American counterparts, were never assigned as wingmen to US pilots in missions over the former Yugoslavia. Being bound to higher standards, they could not be counted on to respond to some threats—to anti-aircraft fire emanating from a school or hospital, for example—in the same way that an American pilot would. Whether countries such as Canada and Britain are collectively liable under Protocol One for the actions of US pilots operating

---

Protecting the Rule of Law

It is precisely in moments of crisis or extreme tension that the relevance and value of the law truly come to the fore, because it is at such times that the temptation to justify recourse to means which would at other times be repudiated is at its most insidious. The law of armed conflict was adopted to restrict violence in war and no argument can be advanced to justify repudiating it, no matter how serious the aggression suffered, no matter what the causes espoused by the parties to the conflict and their reasons for taking up arms.

From this point of view, no State or any other party can declare itself to be above the law, whatever cause it may claim to serve. Conversely, no-one can be cast out from the authority and the protection of the law.

Whether it is a question of "war against terrorism" or any other form of conflict, we must take care not to destroy by arms the values that we claim to protect by arms. *"Who will believe in the justice of your war if it is waged without measure?"* wrote François de La Noue, one of the finest captains of Henri of Navarre, the future Henri IV.

François Bugnion, *International Review of the Red Cross*, September 2002.

---

under NATO targeting procedures remains an open question: the prosecutor for the International Criminal Tribunal for the Former Yugoslavia chose not to investigate any of NATO's alleged war crimes. The issue will not arise in Iraq unless Saddam promptly ratifies Protocol One.[2]

Precision-guided munitions give rise to a further complication. When civilians are present, international humanitarian law requires belligerents to use weapons that can distinguish between civilians and combatants; they should therefore use the most accurate weapons available to them. In yet another instance of political and financial cost-benefit analyses intruding into international humanitarian law, the US argues that this imposes an unfair burden on it, given the substantial costs involved in producing smart bombs. Extending the same logic, it could be argued that, because these weapons reduce the number of civilian casualties across a campaign, an attacking force that uses them is entitled to take more risks—since the overall collateral damage will still be less than in a low-tech war. Applying such calculations to rules designed to protect individual human beings is not only inappropriate, but also immoral.

Civilians can be protected only if a distinction is maintained between combatants and non-combatants. This is achieved by offering prisoner of war status to captured combatants who have carried their arms openly and worn a fixed distinctive emblem (usually a shoulder patch). This doesn't always work, especially in conflicts involving irregular forces in poorer countries, and it can certainly be argued that the requirement of a fixed distinctive emblem is inconsistent with modern forms of warfare. But the distinction is most severely threatened by the practice of US special forces, which constitute an increasingly important part of the US military and have, with the apparent support of the Secretary of Defense, taken to wearing civilian clothing. The practice has already been challenged: when the New Zealand Government sent a contingent of commandos to fight in Afghanistan, it refused to allow them to wear civilian clothes—a decision that created considerable friction with the US.

2. Saddam Hussein was captured by US soldiers on December 13, 2003.

Inhumane Weapons

The use of weapons which cause superfluous injury or unnecessary suffering is similarly prohibited. Dum-dum bullets, chemical and biological weapons are banned outright on the basis that the military benefits of their use can never be proportionate to the suffering caused. Other weapons have been banned by most but not all countries. The US refusal to ratify the 1997 Ottawa Landmines Convention can create awkward situations for its allies. In 2001, Canadian soldiers operating in Afghanistan [during a US-led offensive] were ordered by their American commander to lay mines around their camp. When they refused to do so, US soldiers—who were not subject to the same restrictions—laid the mines for them. Depleted uranium, cluster bombs and fuel-air explosives are among the weapons whose legality remains uncertain. Favoured for their armour-piercing abilities, depleted uranium shells leave radioactive residues that might pose health problems for civilians. Given the scientific uncertainty as to the extent of the risk, one would think that humanitarian concerns would prevail unless the uranium made a major military contribution, which it does not. But again, political and financial expediency has influenced the balance between humanitarianism and military necessity, at least for the US.

Although nuclear weapons are not absolutely banned, their use is subject to the normal constraints of international humanitarian law. It is difficult to see how the use of a nuclear weapon could ever avoid causing suffering disproportionate to military gain. But in March 2002, the Pentagon issued a *Nuclear Posture Review* that cited the need for new nuclear weapons designed to destroy deeply buried command centres and biological weapon facilities. . . . The British Defence Secretary, Geoff Hoon, stated that the UK [United Kingdom] reserves the right to use nuclear weapons against Iraq in 'extreme self-defence'. The basis for Hoon's assertion is a 1996 advisory opinion of the International Court of Justice in which the Court held that it could not 'conclude definitively whether the threat or use of nuclear weapons would be lawful or unlawful in an extreme circumstance of self-defence, in which the very survival of a state would be at stake'. The latter part of this quotation, which Hoon omitted, shows that his reliance on the opinion is misplaced. The only state whose survival might be at stake today is Iraq.

The Threat of Reprisals

Hoon's advisers would do better to direct him to the rules concerning belligerent reprisals: actions that would normally be violations of international humanitarian law but which become legally justifiable when taken in response to violations of the law by the other side. The purpose of reprisals is to deter further violations; the possibility of their use is often pointed to as the reason countries comply with international humanitarian law. Belligerent reprisals, however, must be proportionate to the original violation, and cannot be directed towards civilians or objects indispensable to the survival of civilians.

No treaty specifically prohibits belligerent reprisals carried out with otherwise prohibited weapons. This raises the possibility that it might be legal to use nuclear weapons in response to the use of chemical or biological weapons. In 1991, James Baker, then Secretary of State, privately warned [Iraqi leader Saddam Hussein] that any recourse to chemical or biological weapons would result in a tactical nuclear response. Today, the [George W.] Bush Administration has shown no compunction about making the same threat publicly. *The National Strategy to Combat Weapons of Mass Destruction*, released December [2001], 'reserves the right to respond with overwhelming force—including through resort to all of our options—to the use of WMD against the United States, our forces abroad, and friends and allies'. But the use of any nuclear weapon, even as a reprisal, would almost certainly cause disproportionate civilian suffering, and thus be illegal under standard, non-utilitarian conceptions of international humanitarian law.

The military power of the United States will undoubtedly prevail in Iraq.[3] Reluctant allies will likely be coerced into

3. The United States and its supporters invaded Iraq in March 2003 when Saddam Hussein failed in the eyes of the United States, Great Britain, and other nations to destroy its weapons of mass destruction. The Bush Administration declared the military phase of the war over in May 2003. As of June 2004, casualties at the hands of Iraqi insurgents continue among US and coalition forces remaining in Iraq.

providing practical and political support. And most critics will be silenced, not just by the victory, but also by the fact that only a few thousand civilians will have been killed. But determining the appropriate balance between military necessity and humanitarian concerns has never been the exclusive province of Donald Rumsfeld and his friends. Most international humanitarian law conventions contain something called the Martens Clause, which in its original form was drafted by the Russian delegate to the Hague conferences of 1898 and 1907:

> Until a more complete code of the laws of war is issued, the high contracting Parties think it right to declare that in cases not included in the Regulations adopted by them, populations and belligerents remain under the protection and empire of the principles of international law, as they result from the usages established between civilised nations, from the laws of humanity, and the requirements of the public conscience.

International humanitarian law is in part what you and I and the rest of the people on this planet determine it to be. As war approaches, we should insist that the United States uphold the strict standards of international humanitarian law, not because it is expedient, but because it is the right thing to do.

"[The United States] has rejected agreements that could be interpreted as contrary to key aspects of U.S. military doctrine."

The United States Should Reject Strict International Laws of War

David B. Rivkin and Lee A. Casey

In the following viewpoint David B. Rivkin and Lee A. Casey contend that the United States should reject strict international rules of war designed to make combat more humane. According to the authors, traditional rules of war balanced military necessity and humanitarian concerns, but the new international rules are based on a peacetime policing model that restricts America's ability to conduct war. Moreover, they argue, the strict rules leave U.S. military forces open to prosecution for war crimes. Rivkin and Casey are law partners who have advised the administrations of Ronald Reagan and George H.W. Bush.

As you read, consider the following questions:

1. According to Rivkin and Casey, what is one example of the way the United States shields its soldiers from the dangers of combat?
2. In the authors' view, what principles strike the balance between military necessity and humanitarian considerations?
3. What are the four different sets of legal norms governing the use of armed force, in the authors' view?

War has always had rules, even if only to protect the dead. In *The Iliad*, for example, Homer tells us that Achilles' desecration of Hector's corpse angered the gods. Medieval churchmen sought to limit warfare to certain days of the week and evolved an entire just war theology to constrain the use of armed force. By the Age of Reason, international law "publicists" were busily expounding on the subject, and the 20th century opened with a substantial body of law governing both the right to initiate combat (jus ad bellum) and how armed force is applied (jus in bello). These "laws of war" were based both on custom and treaties and were accepted by all of the Great Powers—including the United States. In more recent years, however, fissures have opened between America and Europe over what the laws of war require with respect to when it is permissible to launch an armed attack, how warfare must be waged, and how the relevant legal norms should be enforced. Today, these disagreements are so fundamental that America and its partners in Europe can be said to operate under different legal codes.

The core of this divergence can be traced to efforts—largely initiated during the Vietnam War era—both to leash the dogs of war and make the laws of combat more humane by mimicking the rules governing domestic police activities, in which deadly force is always the last resort and must not be applied in an "excessive" manner. In the process, "humanitarian" concerns were to be elevated above considerations of military necessity and national interest.

Rejecting the Conventions

These efforts have taken the form of multilateral conventions, such as the 1977 Protocol I Additional to the 1949 Geneva Conventions (Protocol I) or the 1997 Ottawa anti-landmine convention, and of new interpretations of existing treaties (such as the UN Charter), or of customary norms. Although the United States helped to negotiate a number of these treaties, it has steadfastly rejected the most sweeping innovations, favoring instead more traditional jus ad bellum and jus in bello norms. In particular, the United States has clearly asserted that it will use force, where necessary, to defend its interests with or without UN [United Nations] Security Council approval, and has rejected agreements that could be interpreted as contrary to key aspects of U.S. military doctrine.

This reticence is not part of a nefarious American effort to achieve immunity from international law, as critics have sometimes asserted. Unlike many countries, which embrace new international conventions with little intent to comply thereafter, the United States has always taken its obligations seriously—refusing, for example, to ratify treaties it does not plan to implement, whether because of policy or constitutional concerns. What the critics fail to realize is that binding international legal obligations must be based on the consent of the affected states. They cannot be imposed. In eschewing many of the new international legal norms accepted by Europe, the United States has simply acted within its legal rights as an independent sovereign.

The Problem with a Policing Model

Nor does the American refusal to follow Europe's lead in this area stem from any lack of humanitarian zeal. Rather, it can be traced to recognition by the United States that the world remains a dangerous place, and that adoption of a "policing" model for warfare would hamper, if not cripple, America's ability to defend itself—and its allies. Peacetime norms, which guide the conduct of police and security establishments in modern democracies, are far more restrictive than the laws of war because they operate in an environment in which the state has an effective monopoly on the lawful use of force, and in which the damage that any single individual or group can inflict is limited. The laws of war, by contrast, apply in a context in which the state does not have a monopoly on either the lawful right to use force or on the use of the most destructive weapons. War and peace remain different worlds, each with a unique logic and distinct imperatives that require dissimilar rules.

Accepting a "policing" model for warfare would undermine the key tenets of American strategic thinking. For starters, the fundamental American doctrine of "decisive force" would have to go. Any robust use of force is certain to cause some civilian casualties, and, under a model of armed conflict better suited to "managing" problems than winning wars, decisive force would be considered "excessive" and subject to sanction. Similarly, the high value the United States places on force protection would be suspect under these rules. Indeed, one of the principal allegations leveled against the United States is that it has improperly sought to shield its soldiers from the dangers of combat—for example, by operating its aircraft at heights well beyond the range of enemy air defenses, making it difficult in many cases to distinguish between military and civilian targets.

Overall, the importance of this Euro-American doctrinal divergence cannot be overestimated. For the first time in modern history, the principal military powers differ fundamentally over the proper rules governing warfare. . . .

The Traditional Rules of War

Even where the United States and its allies agree that initiating military action is appropriate and lawful, they are rapidly growing apart in their understanding of the all-important rules governing the actual conduct of warfare, the jus in bello. Indeed, because European armed forces have moved toward the "policing" model, in stark contrast to American adherence to the traditional laws and customs of war, transatlantic views on how military operations must be conducted are now quite divergent.

Neither the purpose nor effect of the jus in bello was to forbid the robust use of force. Although the laws of war always included a humanitarian element—as early as the 1580s, Spanish publicist Balthazar Ayala noted that the "intentional killing of innocent persons . . . is not allowable in war"—they were originally developed to benefit soldiers and were shaped by the imperatives of military necessity. The balance between military necessity and humanitarian considerations was struck using the principles of "distinction" (only combatants and military objectives may be targeted for attack) and "proportionality" (the use of force must balance military necessity against the likely damage to civilians or civilian objects).

The overall result was a set of rules that were accepted as a positive good by all civilized states. These rules can be broadly

Excerpts from Protocol I

Article 51: Protection of the Civilian Population

1. The civilian population and individual civilians shall enjoy general protection against dangers arising from military operations. To give effect to this protection, the following rules, which are additional to other applicable rules of international law, shall be observed in all circumstances.

2. The civilian population as such, as well as individual civilians, shall not be the object of attack. Acts or threats of violence the primary purpose of which is to spread terror among the civilian population are prohibited. . . .

4. Indiscriminate attacks are prohibited. Indiscriminate attacks are:

   a. those which are not directed at a specific military objective;
   b. those which employ a method or means of combat which cannot be directed at a specific military objective; or
   c. those which employ a method or means of combat the effects of which cannot be limited as required by this Protocol; and consequently, in each such case, are of a nature to strike military objectives and civilians or civilian objects without distinction. . . .

6. Attacks against the civilian population or civilians by way of reprisals are prohibited.

7. The presence or movements of the civilian population or individual civilians shall not be used to render certain points or areas immune from military operations, in particular in attempts to shield military objectives from attacks or to shield, favor or impede military operations. The Parties to the conflict shall not direct the movement of the civilian population or individual civilians in order to attempt to shield military objectives from attacks or to shield military operations.

Protocol I Additional to the Geneva Convention, 1977.

---

summarized as follows: (1) only sovereign states have the right to make war; (2) civilians cannot be deliberately attacked; (3) combatants can be attacked either en masse or individually; (4) quarter is to be granted when sought; (5) lawful combatants, when taken prisoner or otherwise incapacitated by wounds, are to be accorded the respect and privileges due prisoners of war (POWs); and (6) while all forms of force can be deployed in combat, certain weapons designed to cause unnecessary suffering are proscribed.

This code was tested to the breaking point during the world wars, but its general outline survived and was incorporated into the four Geneva Conventions of August 12, 1949. Like customary jus in bello, the Geneva Conventions neither sought nor purported to interfere with the ability of states to prosecute an armed conflict successfully, and their application did not depend upon the justice of the cause at issue. As explained by the International Committee of the Red Cross (ICRC) in its commentaries on these treaties,

> the application of the Convention does not depend on the character of the conflict. Whether a war is 'just' or 'unjust', whether it is a war of aggression or of defense, the protection and care due to the wounded and sick are in no way affected.

The reasoning behind the practical nature of both customary law and the Geneva Conventions was obvious: a humanitarian "law" that impeded the ability of states to defend their vital interests would, in practice, amount to nothing but a series of pious aspirations. Traditional norms did, therefore, favor established states.

Changing the Rules of War

Efforts to change this began after World War II and were dramatically accelerated in the 1960s and 1970s, in part because of hostility to American involvement in Vietnam. They involved an odd alliance of human rights activists, supporters of "national liberation" movements and Third World governments. While all had different agendas, these groups shared one overarching objective: a desire to "reform" traditional jus in bello norms in ways which would benefit "progressive" non-state entities and handicap traditional state-sponsored military establishments.

Their endeavors, culminating in the 1977 Protocol I Additional to the 1949 Geneva Conventions, were directed at two goals in particular. The first was to revise the longstanding rule that only states can create and utilize military establishments that are legally "privileged" to use force, and the related requirement that all legitimate militaries must organize and operate like "regular" armed forces in order to maintain their "privileged" status. The second was to bestow additional protections from "collateral damage" during war on civilian populations, undermining the ability to wage vigorous combat. The clear import of these reforms was that some military establishments were to be held to higher standards than others. Faced with these developments, the United States has registered strong disagreements with its allies (not to mention numerous NGOs [nongovernmental organizations]) and, while all of Europe's military powers (including Britain, Germany and France) have ratified Protocol I, the United States has not. . . .

The Perils of Protocol I

The new jus in bello norms, reflected in Protocol I and embellished by various academic commentators, have become overly proscriptive and prescriptive. What used to be a few simple normative principles, to be considered by well-trained soldiers when making battlefield decisions, have become something akin to a complex regulatory code to be applied by lawyers on a case-by-case basis, with the full benefit of hindsight. Many of Protocol I's key provisions are phrased in terms like doing "everything feasible", or taking "all feasible precautions", or acting "to the maximum extent feasible." Such terminology defies objective definition, making it all but impossible to assess compliance at the time any particular action is taken. Open-ended legal proscriptions are bad enough in the context of human endeavors in peacetime; they are particularly pernicious in the confusing and confused context of combat, where human judgment is stressed to the utmost and the fog of war reigns. The treaty thus leaves all military forces in combat of any kind open to allegations that they have violated its requirements, for no vigorous combat action could ever comply with Protocol I's strictures. In fact, the only certain way to comply with the treaty is simply to avoid armed conflict altogether.

Protocol I's potential to benefit practitioners of "asymmetric" warfare, not to mention downright criminals, has not gone unnoticed. Both Palestinian militants and Saddam Hussein's Iraq have deliberately placed their own civilians in harm's way in the hope that Israeli or U.S. forces accidentally kill them. (This is particularly the case since Protocol I has also been interpreted to require a higher standard for attacking targets protected by "human shields" than traditional jus in bello norms.) For Hussein, efforts to cause civilian casualties formed part of a systematic strategy, wherein schools, hospitals and mosques, as well as protected symbols like the Red Cross and Red Crescent, were employed for military advantages. Hence, international legal norms that were designed to protect civilians are now serving as an incentive for tyrants and terrorists to endanger their lives. One commentator fittingly called such tactics "lawfare.". . .

Inflexible Restraints

In the past, jus in bello norms reflected a proper balance of humanitarian and military imperatives as well as the consent of sovereign states. They also were predicated upon the principle of reciprocity, enforced by national institutions, and backed up by the availability of reprisals to punish and deter noncompliance. Today, a combination of legal, ethical and political imperatives have rendered ever more elaborate laws of war both inflexible and liable to enforcement by increasingly politicized international institutions.

Legal restraints are also becoming increasingly one-sided, and primarily affect the United States and those few of our allies that continue to take warfare seriously. Plainly said, we now have virtually four different sets of legal norms governing the use of armed force: the traditional strictures, subscribed to by the United States and some of its allies; the policing model, embraced primarily by the Europeans and Canadians; the more permissive norms, which eschew many of the post–World War II developments, embraced by Russia, China, India and a few others; and the "anything goes" approach, with the particular emphasis on the deliberate attacks on civilians practiced by the rogue states and terrorist organizations like Al-Qaeda, Hamas and Hizballah.

Given this overall context, it is all the more regrettable that the fundamental differences between the United States and its allies—over when military force may be lawfully used, how it must be applied properly and who should enforce the norms—show no signs of abatement. These have already led to misunderstandings, tension and outright anger on both sides of the Atlantic and have proven to be highly counterproductive. Franco-German insistence that UN authorization was necessary before military action could be taken against Iraq did not forestall the attack on Saddam Hussein [in 2003], but it nearly wrecked the Security Council. Similarly, assertions that the ICC [International Criminal Court] can investigate, prosecute and punish Americans, whether the U.S. government has ratified the treaty or not, have not led the United States to accept the court's authority. Rather, they have prompted a determined and increasingly successful U.S. effort to obtain from dozens of countries Article 98 agreements guaranteeing that Americans will not be surrendered to the ICC. Efforts to secure overly stringent rules of engagement and other unrealistic jus in bello norms have strained alliance cohesion and impaired the military effectiveness of coalition warfare.

Accepting Differing Principles

Continuing to pretend that these are just minor problems or occasional disputes that can be papered over or resolved through adroit diplomacy is counterproductive. It is imperative to grasp the nature of the problems we face and their full implications. This is particularly true because so much of the European challenge to the American way of war is couched in legal and ethical terms.

The continued perpetuation of legal and moral confusion could eventually erode the American public's consensus supporting any future use of force, and threaten U.S. security and national interests. Hence, it is necessary to make reaffirmation of the traditional laws of war, rules that appropriately balance humanitarian imperatives and the demands of military necessity, an American priority. Ideally, a vigorous U.S. effort to reestablish the traditional jus in bello and jus ad bellum, and restore the role of sovereign states in both developing the substantive norms and upholding them, would bear fruit.

Alternatively, the United States and its allies can simply acknowledge that, because of the policy choices they have made in accordance with differing principles, they are now subject to different international law norms. While Americans cannot expect Europeans to ignore the commitments they have made,

Europeans cannot expect the United States to comply with rules it has not accepted. This does not mean that joint action and operations are impossible, but it does mean that the range of areas in which U.S. and allied forces can act together has narrowed. The result must inevitably be more American "unilateralism", louder choruses of European opposition, and the steady deterioration of a once ideologically consistent alliance. Yet, even this would be preferable to an American embrace of the policing model of warfare, which would impair our ability to prevail in combat. At a time when our way of life is again besieged by violent and unscrupulous adversaries, such a turn of events borders on the suicidal.

"[The International Criminal Court] will have much greater weight if the most powerful nation on earth stays engaged."

The United States Should Join the International Criminal Court to Pursue War Crimes

Jonathan F. Fanton

The United States should support the International Criminal Court (ICC), argues Jonathan F. Fanton in the following viewpoint. The ICC—a permanent tribunal to prosecute in-dividuals accused of genocide, war crimes, and crimes against humanity—is designed to ensure fair trials. For example, the ICC has adopted due process standards similar to those used in the United States, claims Fanton. U.S. opposition to the ICC, he asserts, puts America at odds with nations whose as-sistance it needs in the fight against terrorism. Fanton is a board member of Human Rights Watch, an organization that investigates and exposes human rights violations.

As you read, consider the following questions:
1. In Fanton's view, when did the ICC gain special urgency?
2. According to the author, when will the ICC step in to prosecute war crimes?
3. How can the United States exert its influence even if it does not ratify the treaty, in the author's opinion?

S o many nations are violently at odds with one another that reason for optimism is becoming ever harder to find. Yet on [April 11, 2002,] there was just such a moment: The treaty for the International Criminal Court [ICC] received the ratification it needs to go into effect.

At a dignified ceremony at the United Nations in New York, representatives of several small countries filed papers certifying that their governments have ratified the treaty. That lifted the number of nations that have done so to more than 60, the number necessary for this important new international institution to begin operations.

An Achievement for Human Rights

This is a remarkable achievement: the most important human rights institution created in the last half century.

To reach this point, the treaty has needed two levels of approval. The first came at a 1998 meeting of governmental representatives in Rome when 120 nations signed the document, a number that ultimately grew to 139.

That started the second approval process in which representatives of the governments of at least 60 additional nations also had to formally ratify it. The United States did not sign the treaty at the Rome meeting, largely on the grounds that U.S. soldiers or civilians could be subjected to politically motivated prosecutions.

But President [Bill] Clinton, in the last days of his administration—and despite calling the treaty flawed—decided to sign on. It was a reasonable move, if only because it allowed the U.S. to remain engaged in shaping this new institution.

Even though it has signed, the U.S. is not expected to ratify the treaty any time soon. The assumption had been that Washington would wait to see how the court operates before moving forward.

Undermining the New Court

But now it appears that President [George W.] Bush is considering the unprecedented step of revoking the U.S. signature on the treaty. [Bush revoked the U.S. signature on May 8, 2002.]

That would put the U.S. sharply at odds with its closest

allies. Britain, France, Germany, and Canada have all ratified the treaty and are urging the U.S. to do the same.

At a time when Washington is asking for law enforcement cooperation against terrorism, it hardly seems the moment to undermine an historic new law institution to deal with crimes that are every bit as heinous.

The International Criminal Court

Number of countries that need to ratify the treaty creating the International Criminal Court (ICC) before the court goes into effect	60
Number of countries that have ratified the ICC, as of April 2002	66
Number of countries that signed the Rome Treaty creating the ICC	120
Number of German Nazi officers tried by the Nuremberg Tribunal for committing war crimes during World War II	22
Number of Nuremberg defendants ultimately executed	11
Number of Japanese defendants tried by a Tokyo tribunal for committing war crimes during World War II	28
Number of Tokyo defendants ultimately executed	7

Issues & Controversies, May 10, 2002.

The court's concept is simple. It establishes a permanent tribunal to prosecute individuals—not nations—accused of genocide, war crimes, and of crimes against humanity.

The idea for such a court reaches back to the early days of the 20th Century. It gained special urgency as the century concluded against the backdrop of massacres in Rwanda, Cambodia and the Balkans.

On the one hand, it is hard to imagine taking a position against an institution that could help prosecute future Pol Pots and Saddam Husseins.[1]

1. Under the dictatorial Khmer Rouge regime of Pol Pot, a Cambodian political leader, executions and famine killed an estimated 3 million people. Iraqi leader Saddam Hussein used murder, torture, and rape to maintain his power and led campaigns that resulted in the murder of one hundred thousand Iraqi Kurds.

But that is precisely what appears to be happening when the U.S. stands alongside Libya as the only two nations speaking out against the court.

Safeguarding Against Abuse

Largely with American concerns in mind, the court has been designed to prevent its being used for unfair prosecutions. For example, the International Criminal Court will step in only if a nation fails to carry out investigations and—if appropriate—prosecutions, of crimes that fall under the court's jurisdiction.

Good-faith efforts to discover the truth and hold accountable those who are accused will prevent the court from intervening. When individuals are brought before the court they will receive the highest standards of due process and fair trial guarantees, including the right to counsel, the right to remain silent, the presumption of innocence, and the right to multiple appeals.

These safeguards, of course, still depend on the quality and expertise of the people who are applying them. That is why it is so important for the U.S. to stay engaged with the court.

Even as a nation that has not ratified the treaty, the U.S. can exert influence over selection of prosecutors and judges and, equally important, the creation of the court's culture.

The positive influence of the U.S. in setting up the tribunals dealing with allegations of war crimes, genocide, and crimes against humanity in the former Yugoslavia and Rwanda was significant. The same could hold true for the International Criminal Court—but only if the U.S. participates.

The International Criminal Court will begin to function with or without U.S. participation, but it will have much greater weight if the most powerful nation on earth stays engaged. It would be a mistake for President Bush to isolate the U.S. by removing its signature from the treaty.

Many nations of the world have worked hard to bring themselves to this moment of celebration. By staying involved in the International Criminal Court, even if only by leaving this nation's signature on the treaty, the U.S. will stay on the right side of history.

> *"The US has justifiable concerns about an unrealistic reading of the law of armed conflict . . . because of . . . its unique international responsibilities."*

The United States Should Not Join the International Criminal Court to Pursue War Crimes

Ruth Wedgwood

In the following viewpoint Ruth Wedgwood asserts that the United States should not join the International Criminal Court. Methods the United States might in good faith use to conduct war may subject it to criminal action, she argues. Different nations conduct wars differently, she claims, and thus what each nation considers legitimate means during wartime is subject to interpretation. Wedgwood, a professor of international law at Yale and Johns Hopkins universities, specializes in international crimes and tribunals.

As you read, consider the following questions:
1. According to Wedgwood, how did the principles of discrimination and proportionality shift from World War II to Kosovo, Yugoslavia?
2. In the author's view, what is the problem with the buffer called complementarity?
3. Why is the International Criminal Court unnecessary, in the author's view?

A tour of the Hague recalls history's ambitions for international courts. Andrew Carnegie's Victorian "Peace Palace," with its formal gardens and imposing roof, houses the International Court of Justice. The ICJ's docket of state-to-state complaints in civil cases includes matters such as maritime boundaries, land borders, and questions of state responsibility. There is no compelled jurisdiction; states must agree to the methods by which cases are referred, and the court must rely on the United Nations Security Council to enforce its decisions. But the ICJ is useful to states parties as a way to turn down the volume in fractious disputes, giving governments an occasion to defer provocative issues and yield to compromise. The civil court and its predecessor have not stopped wars; the international court's forebear—a "permanent" court of justice—collapsed in World War II. But the Peace Palace survived the war, and the ICJ has since done an increasing volume of business.

The Hague Tribunals

A less magnificent venue up the road houses the UN Tribunal for the former Yugoslavia, established [in May 1993] to address the crimes of the Balkan wars. The UN Security Council used its extraordinary powers to create this special-purpose tribunal to prosecute the atrocities committed in Bosnia, Croatia, and as it later turned out, Kosovo. The court has enjoyed strong American backing and has made measured progress, convicting 31 defendants. The centerpiece is the trial of Slobodan Milosevic for terrorist attacks against civilians in three nationalist wars. Handed over by Serbian Prime Minister Zoran Djinjic after Belgrade's defeat in the NATO [North Atlantic Treaty Organization] air campaign in 1998, Milosevic has since tried to use the courtroom for his own political purposes. But he is clearly flailing in the face of changed regional politics. The Yugoslav tribunal has had to create a distinctive procedure acceptable to both civil-law and common-law countries and has explored a number of thorny legal and moral issues. One such question involves the degree to which factors like duress and state of mind contribute to the commission of war crimes. Yet the Yugoslav tribunal's work did not deter the ongoing atrocities of the Balkan conflicts; the autocrats who sponsored the Srebrenica massacre and ethnic cleansing in Kosovo were fully aware of the tribunal's jurisdiction. The hope is that the prosecutions will have an effect on other leaders contemplating a career in nationalist violence. Charged by the UN Security Council with the further task of supervising prosecutions connected to the 1994 genocide in Rwanda, the Hague tribunal tries to craft common standards for the Yugoslav trial chambers and a UN sister court in Tanzania.

The Hague also hosted a trial involving the 1988 Libyan-sponsored bombing of Pan Am Flight 103. With terrorism, as with war crimes, "giving it to the lawyers" has been part of a strategy of deterrence. After years of negotiation with Libya and sanctions imposed through the UN Security Council, an agreement was reached to convene a so-called "mixed" tribunal to try two suspects in the bombing. The eight-month trial began in May 2001 at a nearby military base, with Scottish judges applying Scottish law (since the bomb had detonated in Scottish airspace over the town of Lockerbie). A vigorous trial defense and the court's split verdict demonstrated just how hard it is to gather usable courtroom evidence on terrorist networks. Even as the conviction of Abdelbaset Ali Mohmed al Megrahi, a Libyan intelligence agent, made it clear that Tripoli was involved in the civilian murders, Col. Muammar el-Qaddafi was effectively protected.

A Permanent Criminal Court

Finally, The Hague has now offered to take aboard yet a fourth tribunal, the so-called permanent International Criminal Court, created by a treaty agreement negotiated at Rome in 1998. The revival of a permanent criminal court, a fifty-year-old idea, is rooted in our shared dismay at the decade past. Ethnic cleansing and deliberate attacks upon civilians seemed unimaginable in a post-Maastricht Europe. The genocide in Rwanda rattled a world that had supposed such ethnic ferocity was irrational. The ICC is designed to hear cases of serious war crimes, genocide, crimes against humanity, and—in the future—cases of alleged aggression. The court came into formal existence this past summer

[2002]. The choice of 18 judges and a prosecutor is slated for February 2003. European capitals are busily culling their ranks of law professors, prosecutors, ministers, and judges to propose candidates. It should come as no surprise that politics has something to do with the choices, even for a court that purports to abolish politics.

ICC participants may also discover that voice votes in the midst of a UN conference are easier to win than formal treaty ratifications. Of the UN's 189 members, some 81 states had ratified the ICC treaty at the time this article went to press. A significant number of major military powers and regional leaders remain outside the treaty regime, including China, India, Japan, Pakistan, Indonesia, Malaysia, Egypt, Israel, Kenya, and Chile. The Russian Federation is "studying" the matter. Relatively few countries in Asia and Africa have ratified. The commitment to govern national military operations by the decision making of an as-yet-unknown court has inspired caution in more than a few capitals.

Examining American Concerns

This leaves the question of the United States, which has not ratified the treaty. Some unhappy critics have attributed American skepticism about the court to supposed ambitions for empire or hegemony, or a headstrong pursuit of unilateralism. The inference is unfair. Washington has well-grounded and rational concerns about the ICC, its structure, and how its operations could affect the execution of America's responsibilities around the globe, particularly its efforts to maintain strategic stability in key regions, including (in the long term) Europe. Parliamentarians who talk in private to their own military lawyers and senior commanders may discover that even some Europeans share concerns about the effect of the court on military planning.

In war fighting and peace enforcement, there is an acknowledged need to balance restraint and efficacy. Military law is designed to spare civilians from war's cruelties, while permitting countries to protect their citizens. There are some clear "no-go" lines in the conduct of any conflict—"red lines" that any responsible commander will not cross. The norms against massacres are part of the customs of war and do not depend for their mandatory force on any treaty rule or UN mandate. Some matters in legitimate warfare, however, are harder to regulate with bright-line rules. Peace enforcement includes operational norms that are often contentious in practical application.

The Hague Standards

Scholars distinguish between two different spheres of the law of armed conflict—so-called Geneva law and so-called Hague law (each named after the treaty venue that first enunciated the norms). Geneva law protects groups that are *hors de combat*, such as women, children, the sick and wounded, and surrendered soldiers. Most of its rules are widely accepted, and have plain application—at least in traditional conflicts. Hague law, rather, concerns the difficult operational choices to be made on the battlefield and in air campaigns. Hague standards are often closer to principles than to rules; they involve questions of balancing that are morally uncertain and factually sensitive.

The first Hague norm concerns "discrimination"—safeguarding the distinction between military assets and civilian objects. Any well-trained soldier knows that only military targets can be destroyed. The difficulty arises in defining military objects. A second Hague norm concerns "proportionality"—in an attack on military targets, incidental harm to civilians must be limited. It is easy to inscribe such norms on paper. But in the planning and execution of a military campaign, in landscapes where military and civilian sectors share a common infrastructure, both principles prove harder to apply.

Adapting Principles to Real Life

NATO's air campaign in Kosovo gives some striking examples of the difficulty of adapting Hague norms to real-life combat situations. What should qualify as a military target? NATO lawyers exhaustively discussed whether and how to strike at Yugoslavia's oil refineries, electrical grids, television and radio transmission towers, port facilities, railroad spans, and highway bridges. In the legal doctrine of World War II, each of these objects was classified per se as a military target.

There are practical reasons why attacks on infrastructure still remain a part of military planning. Safety for allied aircraft and pilots requires shutting down an adversary's anti-aircraft radar, and air dominance is necessary for ground campaigns as well as air campaigns. Yet even smart weapons may not find mobile anti-aircraft units that are hidden under the lee of a hill; their radar links may most practicably be countered by disabling the adversary's electrical grid. So, too, cutting off the adversary's oil and gas supplies is the most reliable way to immobilize his battle tanks and fighting vehicles, including armored personnel carriers. In cloudy weather and hilly terrain, against an adversary skilled at camouflage, battle armor can be extremely hard to find and target directly. Likewise, there are tactical reasons for damaging highway and rail bridges, to prevent the resupply of ammunition and fresh troops, and to limit the adversary's freedom of maneuver.

The moral difficulty in targeting is that the same transportation infrastructure and energy sources may sustain the civilian community as well. It is exceedingly difficult to fight effectively against an adversary's armed forces without also causing unwanted hardship to the civilian population. The measures taken in Kosovo were part of an effort to counter the Serb campaign of ethnic cleansing—to protect Kosovar Albanians from the depredations of Serb nationalist paramilitaries. The plangent dilemma of balancing harms is not limited to the Balkans.

Conducting an Effective Campaign

Some academic commentators would like to imagine a perfect method of warfare, with complete success in pinpoint strikes that directly disable an adversary's mobile military forces. Other commentators would like to shelter all portions of a country's infrastructure in an armed conflict, regardless of how this prolongs the fighting. Some would like to hold military commanders to a duty of "just-in-time" targeting—waiting until the very moment the adversary proposes to use a particular bridge or railroad. But military commanders who are thwarted by real-life weather, terrain, strategic deception, and mobile weapons may conclude that an effective campaign requires striking at the underlying military infrastructure, including an adversary's energy sources and transportation system.

American commanders are trained to take their ethical and legal responsibilities with great seriousness. The American military sends judge-advocates to the field to advise area commanders on targeting decisions and choice of weapons. They consult computer analyses of possible collateral damage to minimize the harm to civilians. Commanders engage in debate within alliance structures, and American military planners, treatise writers, and trainers also engage with their counterparts. The debates even continue amid the urgent circumstances of a perilous conflict. But one should not assume that the clarity and specificity of criminal law easily fits some of the choices that must be made.

Many countries engage in international peacekeeping under UN or regional auspices. The classical model of peacekeeping demands that troops be deployed only where the conflicting parties have agreed to the mission, where neutrality can be maintained, and where minimal force need be used. Countries as diverse as Fiji, Guatemala, Estonia, India, Pakistan, and Bangladesh, as well as our NATO allies, have made valuable contributions to peacekeeping. The decision of the German Constitutional Court now permits Germany to engage in these missions, with the permission of the Bundestag.

By contrast, "peace enforcement" has few takers. It is the task of a very few countries that have the economic power to pay for the necessary military capability, and a historical role acceptable to their neighbors. The term "peace enforcement" was offered by former UN Secretary General Boutros Boutros-Ghali in his important *Agenda for Peace* to describe the necessarily robust use of military power to displace an aggressor or turn back an invasion. Because of history, Japan and Germany—the world's second and third largest economies—are still hesitant to participate in such missions. Europe has under-invested in military capacity, some would claim. And in its commitment to regional peace, Europe is undecided about a broader global role.

The US faces a number of crucial and hazardous military tasks in which it may have few operational allies. These include the defense of South Korea, strategic stability in the Taiwan Straits, balance in the Middle East, and measures against international terrorism. NATO allies may or may not choose to share in these responsibilities. With a commitment to maintaining security in key areas of the world, Washington is logically concerned with preserving realistic standards for military operations. Innovative proposals for new battlefield standards and the use of advanced technology to save innocent lives will always warrant serious discussion among responsible governments, humanitarian agencies, religious thinkers, military analysts, political commentators, and the public. But they do not routinely belong in the escalated rhetoric of a criminal tribunal. With 220,000 military personnel serving in overseas deployment, it is not surprising that Washington should be cautious about the ICC's broad wingspan.

No Right to a Fair Trial

Rights that Americans take for granted would be greatly diluted or absent entirely in ICC [International Criminal Court] trials. For example, there is no right to a trial by an impartial jury. A verdict is rendered by majority vote of a panel of appointed judges. Thus, a 3-2 vote could doom a defendant to a lengthy prison term—in some cases even a life term.

If that were not bad enough, some—perhaps all—of the judges on a panel might come from countries where there is no concept of an independent judiciary or a tradition of fair trials. A defendant could even face jurists who were officials in regimes that were openly biased against his government or political movement.

Ted Galen Carpenter, *CATO Institute: Daily Commentary*, December 27, 2000.

As witting political observers know, an adversary can characterize the law opportunistically, trying to hobble an act of self-defense or humanitarian intervention. At the beginning of the Kosovo air campaign, Slobodan Milosevic sent his lawyers to the International Court of Justice, charging in a civil suit that almost all of NATO's combat methods were forbidden. Indeed, the Kosovo air campaign was reviewed by the UN tribunal for the former Yugoslavia, and no criminal investigation was opened. But it is worth recalling that this particular tribunal was the creation of the UN

Security Council, in coordination with NATO's goal of stopping ethnic cleansing. The scope of the ICC is far broader. It will hear complaints from a host of countries, organizations, and individual sources. It operates outside the UN's existing security architecture, independent of the UN Security Council. Moreover, its judges are not required to have any experience in military operations or military law, even though the ICC's competence would encompass both the contested issues of Hague law and the clearer standards of Geneva law. A jurist's view on how to balance operational efficacy and unavoidable civilian hazards may be subtly influenced by unspoken beliefs about the necessary role of military strength in protecting societies against intimidation.

Protecting Human Rights

The American interest in framing intelligent standards for the use of force extends to issues such as humanitarian intervention and preemption of terrorist networks, as well as to the role of regional organizations in Africa and elsewhere. The addition of the crime of "aggression" to the ICC's docket may thwart the very forms of intervention that are supported by the human rights community. Though aggression was a historical crime that fit the Nazi war machine in the context of the Nuremberg Trials, the label can also be mobilized for sharply contested political ends. Some ICC supporters say that this part of the court's docket is purely symbolic. Yet even now, some treaty states propose displacing the UN Security Council from its central role in evaluating aggression. Legitimate acts of humanitarian protection or anticipatory self-defense could be jeopardized by a reckless definition of the crime.

Each ally is free to posit a cure for transatlantic irritations. But the ICC controversy deserves to be analyzed on its own merits, not as part of a mélange of transatlantic concerns that includes global warming, steel exports, or the relationship of NATO to the EU [European Union]. It also does not advance common understanding to assume that an interlocutor is proceeding in bad faith. Some European critics would ascribe US concerns about the ICC to a heedless desire to operate without norms or limits. But, as described above, the US has justifiable concerns about an unrealistic reading of the law of armed conflict, indeed because of the very asymmetry of military power in the world and its unique international responsibilities.

It is reasonable to point out that the ICC statute has some safeguards that attempt to prevent misuse of the court's powers. "Complementarity" requires the court to defer to national decisions about war crimes, unless the particular state is "unwilling or unable genuinely" to investigate or prosecute an allegation. Where there are good-faith doctrinal differences, this is no protection. For example, the US will by definition be unwilling to prosecute its pilots or military commanders for carrying out missions that it believes to be lawful.

When there are doubts about a proposal or a new institution, the usual course of action is to watch and see how it works in practice. The stars have not been in alignment here. As both Democrats and Republicans in Congress have noticed, there is no safe "look-over" period. The insistence that the court should have power over third-party countries, even without Security Council decision, is of deep concern to lawmakers. Washington's bipartisan view is that the ICC has no right to claim jurisdiction over the citizens of a state that has chosen not to ratify the treaty without the Security Council's concurrence. This was the view taken by President [Bill] Clinton when he signed the treaty on December 31, 2000, and it is a view shared by the Democratic Senate, the Republican House of Representatives, and President George W. Bush. One may or may not agree with some of Washington's methods of pursuing the point, but it is just as well that ICC treaty states not labor under any misapprehension about the importance of the issue to the US. There will be plentiful work for the ICC docket in the exercise of more traditional theories of jurisdiction.

A More Palatable Criminal Court

Constructive things can be done, even at present, to help mend the relationship between the ICC and the US. It would be useful if some of the judges nominated to the court were chosen from among military lawyers and judge advocates, to bring some practical judgment and military experience to the court's deliberations. So, too, the appointment of deputy prosecutors should include people with a working background in Hague law, as well as more traditional international and criminal lawyers. (One could even be daring and choose an American.) The court may also wish to have a roster of military experts chosen from responsible militaries for use as expert witnesses. Secondly, the new ICC prosecutor may wish to announce guidelines for case selection. The experience of the Yugoslav and Rwanda tribunals has shown that international courts can only handle a limited caseload, and constructive engagement in undisputed areas could be reassuring. Thirdly, it would be within the prosecutor's prerogative to clarify the components of decisions on complementarity, in particular, to make clear that the court will apply the European idea of deferring to good-faith national interpretations of the law of armed conflict, with a "margin of appreciation."

The NATO alliance and other coalitions for peace enforcement will require practical standards for joint operations in the future. A coordinated defense requires planning, reasonable interoperability, and, not least, a workable consensus on what the law allows. Thus, a continuing North Atlantic conversation on the legal and ethical principles that govern the use of armed force is in our common interest. Our current differences on the modes of enforcement should not distract us from the ambition of our shared normative commitments.

Periodical Bibliography

The following articles have been selected to supplement the diverse views presented in this chapter.

Kenneth Anderson	"Who Owns the Rules of War?" *On the News: Crimes of War Project*, April 24, 2004. www.crimesofwar.org.
BusinessWeek Online	"Time to Rewrite the Rules of War?" April 1, 2003. www.businessweek.com.
Michael Byers	"Prisoners on Our Conscience," *Guardian Weekly*, January 17, 2002.
Ted Galen Carpenter	"No Civil Liberties at the International Criminal Court," *CATO Institute: Daily Commentary*, December 27, 2000.
Dennis P. Chapman	"Treachery and Its Consequences: Civilian Casualties During Operation Iraqi Freedom and the Continued Utility of the Law of Land Warfare," *Armor*, January/February 2004.
G. Russell Evans	"Why Terrorist Detainees Are Not POWs" *NewsMax*, February 11, 2002.
Richard J. Goldstone	"International Law and Justice and America's War on Terrorism," *Social Research*, Winter 2002.
Christopher Greenwood	"International Law and the 'War on Terrorism,'" *International Affairs*, April 2002.
Anthony E. Hartle	"Atrocities in War: Dirty Hands and Noncombatants," *Social Research*, Winter 2002.
Hendrik Hertzberg	"Collateral Damage," *New Yorker*, April 7, 2003.
Eric S. Krauss and Mike O. Lacey	"Utilitarian vs. Humanitarian: The Battle over the Law of War," *Parameters*, Summer 2002.
Stefan Lovgren	"Iraq Conflict: Following the 'Laws of War'?" *National Geographic*, April 4, 2003.
Paul Maliszewski and Hadley Ross	"We Happy Few: The U.S. Soldier's Laws of War in Principle and in Practice," *Harper's*, May 2003.
David Masci	"Ethics of War," *CQ Researcher*, December 13, 2002.

W. Hays Parks   "The United States Military and the Law of War: Inculcating an Ethos," *Social Research*, Winter 2002.

Hugo Slim   "Why Protect Civilians? Innocence, Immunity, and Enmity in War," *International Affairs*, May 14, 2003.

Stuart Taylor   "We Don't Need to Be Scofflaws to Attack Terror," *National Journal*, February 4, 2002.

CHAPTER 4

How Can War Be Prevented?

Chapter Preface

In a speech before the United Nations (UN) on September 12, 2002, President George W. Bush asked, "Will the United Nations serve the purpose of its founding, or will it be irrelevant?" UN critics have begun to question whether the UN can serve its purpose—to prevent war and preserve global security—in an era when rogue states and terrorists can obtain weapons of mass destruction (WMDs). UN supporters, on the other hand, contend that the UN is up to the challenge of maintaining peace and defending international order. In recent years, the United Nations has become central to debates about how war can be prevented.

Fifty-one nations ratified the UN charter on October 24, 1945, shortly before the end of World War II. At the UN's first meeting, Great Britain's King George VI said, "It is for you to lay the foundations of a new world where such a conflict as that which lately brought our world to the verge of annihilation must never be repeated." Now comprised of 191 member nations, the UN General Assembly is responsible for nonbinding resolutions on international issues. The Security Council, the most important arm of the UN, grapples with issues of war and peace. The United States, Great Britain, France, the Russian Federation, and China constitute the council's five permanent members, each with veto power over all decisions. Ten nonpermanent members are elected by the General Assembly to two-year terms. The Security Council dispatches peacekeepers to war-torn countries, authorizes economic and military sanctions against aggressors, and approves the use of force to restore peace. Unlike General Assembly resolutions, those passed by the Security Council are binding on member nations.

UN critics argue that the international body's failure to disarm Iraq—a rogue member nation that the Bush administration claimed was developing WMDs—demonstrates that the UN cannot effectively maintain global security. According to foreign policy analyst Daniel Goure, "Since the early 1950s, [the UN] hasn't lived up to its mandate 'To prevent wars and chase down aggressors.' Recent events just showed how much this is the case." Goure refers to the deadlock within the Security Council over what to do when head UN arms inspector Hans Blix reported back at the end of January 2002 that Iraq "appears not to have come to a genuine acceptance . . . of the disarmament that was demanded of it." The United States and Great Britain wanted UN authorization to use force against Iraq unless it agreed to immediately disarm. France, China, Germany, and Russia wanted arms inspections to continue and threatened to veto any UN resolution authorizing military action. Despite last minute attempts to reach a compromise, the Security Council remained divided when on March 17, 2003, the United States and Great Britain attacked Iraq without UN authorization. The impasse over Iraq, UN critics contend, thus demonstrates the UN's ineffectiveness.

UN supporters disagree with this assessment. The UN has the tools to maintain international order, they contend. According to their views, the Security Council deadlock resulted because some members questioned U.S. claims that Iraq had WMDs, a belief that gained support when U.S. weapons inspectors failed to find WMDs after the March 2003 invasion. Foreign policy analyst Christopher Preble asserts, "The United Nations wouldn't have opposed [U.S.] intervention in Iraq if the majority of member states believed that Iraq was a threat to the U.S. That was the problem: They didn't believe that we were genuinely threatened." Moreover, a Security Council deadlock and the resulting unilateral action of the United States and Great Britain is insufficient to prove that the UN is irrelevant, supporters contend. "Even when you look at Iraq, which was supposed to be the U.N.'s darkest hour, you see evidence that it is terribly relevant," maintains Columbia University professor Edward Luck. "Why has the United States gone back to the United Nations over and over again with regard to Iraq? Because the U.N. is a vital part of the furniture of international relations, and the U.S. knows that," Luck concludes.

The role of the United Nations in maintaining global security and preventing war remains controversial. In the following chapter the authors debate war prevention theories and methods.

> *"A real living peace . . . is attainable and quite possible when built upon the hard work of conflict resolution and diplomacy."*

War Can Be Prevented

Dane Spencer

People will always have conflicting goals and ideas, but conflicts need not lead to war if leaders are willing to resolve conflict diplomatically, claims Dane Spencer in the following viewpoint. Because nearly a hundred million soldiers and civilians have died during late-twentieth-century wars, some believe war is inevitable, but people are not warlike; warlike leaders create wars, asserts Spencer. War can be prevented, he contends, when people realize that peace is not the absence of conflict but a state in which people resolve conflict without violence. Spencer, a landscape architect, is a peace activist.

As you read, consider the following questions:
1. While the military is good at killing, at what is it inept, in Spencer's opinion?
2. According to the author, if it wasn't the destruction of the Twin Towers on September 11, 2001, what caused this country's morale to plummet?
3. What does the author claim it is our human nature to do, if it is not to go to war?

If history is any indication, the United States may be subject to the violence of war within my lifetime. I am 42. Military scholars say that war and its resulting violence on a civilian population is unavoidable. We are told that peace just isn't obtainable in the Middle East, or in other war torn countries across the globe; that violent conflict will always be a fact of life as we try to control territory and natural resources. We are given example after example how, throughout history and including today, violent conflict is inevitable and in some cases necessary.

The War Experts

Some people are quick to defend the notion that there is nothing to be done about civilian death and destruction caused by violent conflict, that in times such as these, war is best left to the experts. It is true that only war experts know how to successfully conduct war, that to win a conflict is to win by any means, and that includes civilian casualties. Talking heads for the military tell us that they are working to reduce the number of civilian casualties through more efficient means of killing—smarter bombs, better technology. But, the truth remains that while any military is good at killing, it is inept at not targeting civilians. After all, to target civilians is to terrorize a population and to attack an enemy's infrastructure. With this illogic, there is no such thing as a non-military target.

Yet, if we leave war to the war experts, who will oversee the peace process? Who are our peace experts? [Vice President] Dick Cheney and [Secretary of Defense] Donald Rumsfeld? They have been buddies since their early thirties, and they have amassed power by putting their friends in important positions throughout the government and the military. They are war experts dictating military policy for this country, yet there is not a diplomat for peace between the two of them. There is no peace equivalent to the Department of Defense, we have no such office or branch of government that we can go to in times such as these. Our nonexistent Department of Diplomacy and Conflict Resolution Services didn't just get an additional $40 billion infusion into an already huge capital, operating, and maintenance budget—that was our Department of War. Blind military spending appears to be a priority for our country, with no visible way to counteract or slow it down. The peace dividend has long since been chucked out the window.

And, what has become of our domestic programs that deal with our children's education; our failing health care system, our weakened social security, our declining environmental health, and our loss of morale as citizens of this country?

It wasn't the destruction of the twin towers on September 11, 2001 and the threat of terrorism that is causing this country's morale to plummet. It is the lack of hope that things will ever get better in the lifetime that is ahead. There is no clear way out, no end in sight.

That is because we are spending billions of dollars on high tech toys of destruction for a group of people who want to see major conflict, so that they can use their toys against military targets, and civilians if necessary. They want to see this conflict happen just like a six-year-old boy with a firecracker wants to see it explode.

The Civilian Casualties

Let the facts speak for themselves: World War II resulted in the killing of 61 million people; 67% of those killed (40 million) were civilian. Violent clashes and wars worldwide for the 1950s resulted in 4.6 million people killed, 50% being civilian (2.3 million). In the 1960s, 6.5 million people were killed; 56% were civilian (3.64 million). The 1970s saw fewer people killed (3 million), but most of them were civilians (2 million). The 1980s saw 5.5 million people killed through violent conflict around the world, with over 4 million being civilian. Conflict and wars of the 1990s left 5 million people killed worldwide; half were civilian. From WWII to 2000 we have seen 85.6 million killed, with 63% of those being civilian (54 million).

The [1991 Persian] Gulf War [in which United Nations forces ejected Iraq from Kuwait after its unlawful invasion] has seen 200,000 casualties, both civilian and military, by the end of the conflict. But, ten years after the end of this conflict, 10,000 American service men and women had died from the Gulf War Syndrome [a medical condition affecting some veterans of the Gulf War]. Of the 600,000 troops that had served in the Gulf War, 230,000 have applied for medical assistance since the end of that conflict. A combination of things are suspected causes of this widespread illness. It is believed that either untested anthrax vaccinations, the transfer of toxic poly-hydrocarbons from plastic packaging of MRE's (meals ready to eat), or troop use of depleted uranium munitions (which was never disclosed to the troops who were using them) have caused severe illness. Whatever the cause, this is a better kill and injury rate than any enemy could hope to level on our troops.

Because of sanctions on Iraq, 500,000 children have died from diarrhea and malnutrition from the lack of clean water, a direct result of targeting civilian infrastructure by the U.S. military.

As technology improves and as dollars increase, the efficiency of killing also improves. But improving the efficiency of killing doesn't reduce the number of civilian deaths, it increases the number of civilian deaths. The number increases because there is a greater tendency to use these weapons on lesser known targets. If it can be claimed that a "smart bomb" (remember bombs are only as smart as the people who use them) can "surgically" remove a military target within tight civilian quarters with minimal civilian casualties, then the tendency to use these weapons in tight civilian quarters will increase, resulting in higher numbers of civilian deaths.

The Myth of Peace

Civilians do not wage war. Indeed, war and military police actions are argued as necessary to protect civilians and civilian infrastructure. So, civilians agree to support the military in promise that the war will not touch them. Civilians are confident that their families will not suffer the losses of their enemies. Most civilians who have experienced war however, come to know that war only means to reduce profits and production, bringing only pain, suffering, and agony down the road. But nonetheless, these civilians have been convinced that their experts have exhausted all other diplomatic avenues and have come up empty handed. The leaders come back to say "Sorry, war is inevitable. Prepare for war," and the civilians feel they have no other choice.

How many times have you heard someone say that it is in our "human nature," to go to war? That the human species is violent and warlike and there is nothing that we can do about it? That might makes right, to the winner goes the spoils?

Facing the World's Bullies

Dealing with a bully without becoming a thug yourself is not wimpish, negative passivity. Active alternatives to violence require a blend of physical courage, emotional maturity, spiritual determination and mental calm, which add up to a wholeness of person. Those who have developed it manifest an unusual, quiet, formidable strength that the US Civil Rights movement called soul-force. It may well be the new power of the 21st century—perhaps the only power which will make us safe and save our lives.

Priscilla Elworthy, *New Internationalist*, September 2003.

To say that it is in our human nature to kill others and that war is inevitable perpetuates the myth that war is forever our way. It is not our nature to kill others who don't agree with us or who think differently from ourselves. But, it is our human nature to be fearful of others who have opposing ideas or who are different from ourselves. This fear may go in two directions: Our fear may sway into curiosity or it may sway into anger and violence.

Another trait of our "human nature" is to divide ourselves into leaders and followers. Leaders can choose to go to war for entire populations and will not hesitate to call upon the followers to do the dirty work. It is not our human nature to go to war, but it is in our human nature to be led into war.

Leading People to Peace

Therefore, if we can be led into war, we can be led into peace.

People are not warlike creatures. It is the random individual who sees value in herding the masses into violence. Every war is led by someone who has convinced a critical mass of people that war is the only option. This is true with either side of any war or violent conflict. And, it is the same for peace. In any conflict that has not escalated into violence or where violence has ceased, a leader has led a critical mass of people to great change.

The war in the Middle East is being perpetuated not because Israel and Arab leaders can't come to an agreement, but because the concept of peace is being used incorrectly. The myth of peace begins within the very roots of the Judeo-Christian religion. Peace in this religious sense is an unattainable time/place. Peace is symbolized by the phrase, "when the lion lays down with the lamb," which indicates that all life on Earth will be as one, living in harmony for the rest of all eternity.

This peace does not exist, nor will it ever exist on this Earth inhabited by our wonderfully fallible human species. Peace is not the cessation of conflict, and a resulting agreement in totality. For the Mideast, the lion may never lay down with the lamb. Peace is a continuing evolving process that produces nonviolent results. Peace can revert to war or it can be sustained through constant communication, but it can never be stagnant or absolute.

Peace begins when violence ends. That doesn't mean that the conflicting ideas will suddenly disappear. It means that when people stop doing violence to each other—stop killing—negotiations can begin. In the simplest terms, peace is a process where no one is dying from an act of aggression. This is a real living peace that is attainable and quite possible when built upon the hard work of conflict resolution and diplomacy. Peace is not a time/place. Peace is a process that is ongoing and never without tension.

"War cannot be eliminated entirely, only avoided by deterrence."

War Cannot Be Prevented

Victor Davis Hanson

War is inevitable, argues Victor Davis Hanson in the following viewpoint. Unfortunately, he claims, the more affluent a nation gets, the more inclined it becomes to believe that war can be prevented. Thus, as nations get richer, they become less willing to support a large military and become less secure. Hanson, a military historian, is author of *Autumn of War: What America Learned from September 11 and the War on Terrorism.*

As you read, consider the following questions:
1. In Hanson's opinion, why does an F-16 fighter jet not exist in a vacuum?
2. What has resulted in the placement of social and cultural limitations on the conditions of battle, in the author's view?
3. According to the author, what should people do with new technologies and new approaches to fighting?

War is eternal. It is part of the human condition; it is, as [Greek philosopher] Heraclitus wrote, "the father of us all." This is the first thing we must remember whenever discussion turns to "revolutions in military affairs." Some things will change, but the underlying laws and lessons that have shown themselves over millennia of warfare remain true about wars today—and wars tomorrow.

Key Truths About War

One of these key truths is that culture largely determines how people fight. The degree to which a society embraces freedom, secular rationalism, consensual government, and capitalism often determines—far more than its geography, climate, or population—whether its armies will be successful over the long term. Israel today is surrounded by a half-billion Middle Eastern Muslims—and has little to fear from their conventional militaries. Kuwait and Saudi Arabia have some of the most sophisticated weapons in the world; Saddam Hussein's Iraq still fields one of the largest armies;[1] Iran boasts of spirited and fiery warriors. Israel—not to mention the United States—could vanquish them all. This appraisal is simply a statement of fact; it is neither triumphalist nor ethnocentric. It recognizes that if—for example—Iraq were to democratize, establish a Western system of free speech and inquiry, and embrace capitalism, then Iraq too, like Taiwan or South Korea, might well produce a military as good as Israel's.

Another key truth is that overwhelming force wins. Much has been made of the latest epidemic of terror and suicide bombing—as if hijackers with tiny budgets could overcome opponents who spend trillions on defense. But history proves otherwise: Frightful terrorists such as the Jewish sicarii of Roman times, the ecorcheurs of the Hundred Years' War, and the Mahdi's dervishes in 19th-century Sudan usually petered out when they were faced with an overwhelming military force that was fighting for attractive ideas. Guerrillas, after all, require money, modern weapons, and bases in countries with friendly governments. Superpowers—such as

1. The U.S. and coalition forces invaded Iraq on March 19, 2003. The regime of Saddam Hussein was officially declared at an end on April 9, 2003.

imperial Rome and contemporary America—have the where-withal to deny the terrorists access to much of this necessary support. [The terrorist attacks of] September 11 [2001] revealed the complacency and carelessness of a democratic and affluent United States; but the relative absence of follow-up attacks—as America systematically eradicates [the fundamentalist Islamic extremist group] al-Qaeda 7,000 miles away from its shores—suggests that a powerful state can more than handle stateless terrorists.

It can do so because a Green Beret [army special forces] fighting terrorists in a cave can rely on a multibillion-dollar carrier battle group to bomb the terrorists; all he has to do is call in his GPS [Global Positioning System] coordinates. This is the West's edge; and a chief military challenge of the 21st century, therefore, will be not terrorists per se, but the degree to which globalization brings the Western way of war to the much larger non-West.

A Military of Qualified Men

During the Clinton administration, it was feared that exported weapons and pilfered expertise might soon bring China technological parity with America. But no one is yet sure whether the simple possession of sophisticated arms amounts to military equivalence—without the accompanying and more fundamental Western notions of discipline, market logistics, free-thinking command, and civilian supervision.

An F-16 fighter jet does not exist in a vacuum: A literate middle class is needed to produce mechanics who can service and modify it; freedom of scholarship is required if designers are going to update it; and an open society is necessary if the plane's sophisticated controls are going to be operated by competent, motivated, and individualistic pilots. As a rule, Israeli pilots proved deadly against Syrian jets in Lebanon—but Iraqis in advanced Russian aircraft would fly into Iran rather than fight American planes during the Gulf War.

Another example: There are probably plenty of Stinger missiles still hidden away in Afghanistan, but it has been nearly two decades since they were built—and Afghans have not modified or updated them to meet the intervening efforts to neutralize their effectiveness. In the short term, such subtle differences don't seem important. But in the long run—as we have seen in the Falklands, the Arab-Israeli wars, the Gulf War, and Afghanistan—they can trump numerical superiority, tactical genius, and heroism itself. There is a reason that [former Palestinian leader Yasir] Arafat, not [Israeli prime minister Ariel] Sharon, was surrounded in his bunker: It is not terrorists, but tanks—and the quality of men in them—that decide the preponderance of strength in the Middle East.

Accepting Responsibility for Defense

This is true not just in the Middle East but everywhere. The education system, therefore, and the preservation of an open society with a common Western culture are as valuable for our national security as our impressive military hardware. If the degree of Westernization in the next few years will often determine which armies win and lose, history also teaches us that with affluence and personal freedom comes a sense of laxity. The fact that a society can, in theory, defeat its enemies does not ensure that it will indeed do so. The unwillingness of affluent individuals to accept the responsibilities of defense is a common theme in Roman authors as diverse as Livy and Juvenal.

Instilling Fear of War's Consequences

To eliminate war the basic causes of conflict among nations must be eliminated. Historically, this has proved impossible, and wars continue. But if the causes of war cannot be eliminated, the best means of decreasing their likelihood is to instill such a tremendous fear of the consequences of war that even aggressive nations would willingly avoid it. Nuclear weapons, it cannot be denied, have instilled this fear of war to an intense degree and thus have served a useful purpose in preventing the all-out war that they have the potential to unleash.

Mark N. Katz, *Air University Review*, July/August 1979.

We see evidence of this sort of smugness in today's Europe, whose elites snicker at America's muscular response to September 11, whose taxpayers are unwilling to shoulder defense expenditures that might imperil their lavish social spending, and whose society has embraced a utopian view that war itself is simply outdated and can be eliminated by properly educated diplomats. (This is in stark contrast to such powerful countries as China and India, which have lately begun to adopt elements of the Western way of war: They maintain large defense establishments and have highly nationalistic citizenries that are not yet affluent or secure enough to trust that war is a relic of the past.)

The United States doesn't share Europe's anti-military bias, but it has its own problems. In a society in which a $50,000, three-ton, gas-guzzling monstrosity is required to transport safely a soccer mom and her twelve-year-old a few blocks to the practice field, it should come as no surprise that the military, too, has an "SUV syndrome": the embrace of expensive gadgetry and machines to ensure at all costs the safety of the individual combatant. The more that technology and science can ameliorate the human condition of the average American citizen, and prolong life by conquering the age-old banes of accident, disease, and famine, the more our cultures expect that our soldiers, too, will avoid wounds and death. The anticipation that we shall all die at 90 in our sleep— peacefully and without pain—results in an array of social and cultural limitations placed upon the conditions of battle. Societies that are affluent and free expect their soldiers to be able to kill thousands of enemies who are neither—and without incurring any deaths in the process. In Afghanistan [in 2001], our military has chosen repeatedly to be wary about exposing our own men to danger—even when it meant that dozens of dangerous al-Qaeda and Taliban [rulers] would escape.

The Tools of War

Another eternal law of war is that the advantage keeps shifting, back and forth, between defense and offense. For centuries the methods of defense—whether stout ashlar-stone walls in the pre-catapult era, or knights in the age before the crossbow—trumped the effectiveness of most attackers. Today, however, destruction is easy—thanks to automatic weapons, precision bombing, and nuclear arsenals. But we may be witnessing the beginning of a shift back toward the defense: Breakthroughs in impenetrable light plastic and composite materials may well make our infantrymen as well protected against projectiles as yesterday's hoplites. We have seen this already in Afghanistan, where unharmed American soldiers have found spent slugs in their ultramodern flak vests.

For all the lethality of bunker-busters, daisy-cutters, and thermobaric bombs, reinforced caves—outfitted with space-age communications and supplies—seemed to protect al-Qaeda warriors well enough to force our designers back to the drawing boards to discover new ordnance that might bore through yards of such rock. On the intercontinental level, the once ridiculed concept of missile defense is no longer so ridiculous, and only a few years rather than decades away—raising the eerie and once inconceivable thought that a missile exchange might not result in horrendous carnage.

Using Timeless Weapons

Tomorrow's wars will also prove that other historical rules remain valid. In the 1970s, for example, it was popular to scoff that carriers were simply floating targets that would "last about a minute" in a war with the Soviet Union. But any weapons system that is mobile, capable of sending out dozens of planes either to attack any type of enemy or to defend their mother ship, has timeless value. Despite its massive size, nuclear propulsion, electronics, and superior design, today's Enterprise is not all that different in form and function from its eponymous ancestor that fought at Midway.[2] Why? Because a floating airstrip is a perfect and timeless weapon, one not dependent on volatile host countries; it is forever mobile, lethal at great distances, and eternally useful because it can be updated to reflect new technologies.

By the same token, submarines that twenty years ago were deemed the wave of future naval warfare have played a less prominent role in the post–Cold War era; their nuclear arsenals and near-miraculous stealth have proved of little value in the asymmetrical Gulf War or the air campaign against Serbia. It would, however, be a mistake to dismiss as superfluous any weapon that can strike without being seen: An array of

2. a mid–Pacific Ocean atoll over and next to which the United States and Japan fought one of World War II's greatest carrier battles, ultimately turning the tide in favor of the United States

conventionally armed submarines has already been modified to fire dozens of cruise missiles at distant inland targets, and there's no reason submarines could not be posted off the coast of Iran or North Korea with a full arsenal of anti-ballistic missiles to ensure that any nukes launched from those countries would be shot down a few thousand feet from their launch pads.

The conventional wisdom of the pundits will always be evanescent. We must not be hoodwinked by their present-ism into thinking that a new weapon or a new theory has "reinvented" war. It cannot happen. There will be new technologies and new approaches to fighting—but we need to see how they fit into age-old military realities.

Preparing for War

The first such reality is that war will not be outlawed or made obsolete. This idea is a spasm of utopian thinking on the part of elites; its only result is to get millions of less educated and less affluent innocents killed. War cannot be eliminated entirely, only avoided by deterrence. "He who wishes peace should prepare for war," runs the ancient wisdom—and it remains true today. When America had a "Department of War," no more Americans were killed overseas than in the period aider its name was changed to the less bellicose "Department of Defense"—reminding us that we can repackage and rename conflict through euphemism and good intentions, but never really alter its brutal essence.

The second key reality is that war is not merely a material struggle, but more often a referendum on the spirit. No nation has ever survived once its citizenry ceased to believe that its culture was worth saving. Themistocles' Athens beat back hundreds of thousands of Persians; yet little more than a century later Demosthenes addressed an Athens that had become far wealthier—and could not marshal a far larger population to repulse a few thousand Macedonians. Rome was larger, far more populous, and wealthier in A.D. 400 than in 146 B.C.—but far more unsure about what it meant to be a Roman, and confused about whether being Roman was better than, or merely different from, being German or Persian. France, which stopped the Germans at Verdun, a quarter-century later let them romp through the Ardennes in six weeks. The more complex, expensive, and lethal our weapons become, the more we must remember that they are still just tools, whose effectiveness depends on the discipline, training, and spirit of their users.

If the United States continues to believe that its culture is not only different from, but better than, those of the rest of the world—and if it believes that its own past pathologies were symptoms of the universal weaknesses of men, rather than lasting indictments of our civilization—we will remain as strong as we were during the wars of the 20th century. In contrast, if we ever come to believe that we are too healthy, too sophisticated, and too enlightened ever to risk our safety in something as primitive as war, then all the most sophisticated weapons of the 21st century will not save us when our hour of peril comes. And, as September 11 reminds us, that hour most surely will come.

| "*Democratic leaders are more careful about the lives of their citizens and, therefore, they fight less severe wars.*"

Fostering Democracy Worldwide Will Prevent War

R.J. Rummel

Fostering freedom will help end wars because nations whose people participate in their own governance are less likely to go to war, argues political science professor R.J. Rummel in the following viewpoint, excerpted from *Saving Lives, Enriching Life: Freedom as a Right and a Moral Good.* The severity of war increases in totalitarian and authoritarian nations because dictators maintain control with coercion and force and thus only avoid war when their enemy is militarily stronger, Rummel asserts. Democracies, on the other hand, share mutual interests and a common culture that encourages diplomacy and discourages costly wars, he maintains.

As you read, consider the following questions:

1. According to Rummel, who was one of the first philosophers to argue that peace lay in creating republics?
2. What much deeper factor than fear of death and destruction is at work in preventing wars among democracies, in the author's view?
3. According to the author, how do dictators manipulate the populace?

R.J. Rummel, *Saving Lives, Enriching Life: Freedom as a Right and a Moral Good.* www.hawaii.edu/powerkills/NOTE15.HTM, January 17, 2001. Copyright © 2001 by Rudy J. Rummel. Reproduced by permission.

All proposals to prevent war have suffered from this defect: they ignore how dictators differ from democratic leaders. There have always been those who when they inherit or seize power, forcefully fill their army with unwilling soldiers, and then grind them to death in a war to grab more power and control over others. The rogues' gallery of these murderers and aggressors is long. . . . When you have such people controlling large armies, the solutions to war, such as pacifism, unilateral disarmament, or disarmament treaties, do not work. They make the world safe only for such tyrants.

The Origin of Democratic Peace Theory

Now, finally, we have the proven knowledge to avoid both wars and the aggression of dictators. This solution was proposed in the latter part of the eighteenth century and recent social science research has shown it so. In his *Perpetual Peace*, written in 1795, the great German Philosopher Immanuel Kant argued that the way to universal peace lay is creating republics, or what today we would call representative democracies. Kant wrote that:

> The republican constitution, besides the purity of its origin (having sprung from the pure source of the concept of law), also gives a favorable prospect for the desired consequence, i.e., perpetual peace. The reason is this: if the consent of the citizens is required in order to decide that war should be declared (and in this constitution it cannot but be the case), nothing is more natural than that they would be very cautious in commencing such a poor game, decreeing for themselves all the calamities of war.

Note two things about this solution. First is that where people have equal rights and freely participate in their governance. they will be unlikely to promote war in which they or their loved ones might die and their property destroyed. And second, where leaders are responsible to their people as voters, they will be unwilling to flight. Then when both leaders of two nations are so restrained, war between them should not occur.

The idea that democracies are therefore inherently peaceful was not lost to others. It became part of a more general philosophy of governance that Kant shared with liberals of the time, a system of belief we now call *classical liberalism*. . . .

Adam Smith, John Stuart Mill, and John Locke, among other influential thinkers of the time, argued for the maximum freedom of the individual. They believed in minimal government. They also supported free trade between nations and, as I noted, a free market within. Such freedom, they argued, would create a harmony among nations, and promote peace. As Thomas Paine—who like most of America's Founding Fathers was a classical liberal—wrote in his influential *Rights of Man* in 1791–1792,

> Government on the old system is an assumption of power, for the aggrandizement of itself; on the new [republican form of government as just established in the United States], a delegation of power for the common benefit of society. The former supports itself by keeping up a system of war; the latter promises a system of peace, as the true means of enriching a nation.

Full proof of this point had to wait, however, until scientists like Bruce Russett, Zeev Maoz, James Lee Ray, and myself, could develop research methods to document it. . . . We did related research throughout the 1970s, thanks in part to the growth of new statistical models made possible by the advent of the computer, and in the 1980s we, and scholars who followed our lead, proved Kant correct. By then we had collected data on all wars that had occurred over the last several centuries, and by applying various statistical analyses to these data, we established that there never has been a war between well-established democracies. Moreover, through these techniques we also proved that there was not a hidden factor accounting for this, such as a lack of common borders, or geographic distance between democracies. Nor was this democratic peace attributable to the wealth of democracies; or their international power, education levels, technology, resources, religion, or population density. Our findings are straightforward: Well-established democracies do not make war on each other. . . .

Explaining Democratic Peace

Why is it that free and democratic peoples do not make war on each other? Remember Immanuel Kant's hypothesis that since you would not want to bear the cost of wars, you would, if you could, restrain your leaders. On the surface, this seems a good explanation, and it does help to explain why democracies do not make war on each other. Yet democratic people have also been jingoistic. They have favored war and encouraged their leaders to fight. For instance, the public outcry over the explosion aboard the American battleship *Maine* in a Cuban harbor and its sinking with a loss of 260 men in 1898 pressured Congress and President [William] McKinley into intervening militarily in Cuba. Spain then reluctantly declared war on the United States. American public opinion also strongly favored President [Harry] Truman's commitment of American troops to the defense of South Korea against the North Korean invasion in 1950; and similarly favored President [Lyndon] Johnson's request to Congress for a blank check—the Tonkin Gulf resolution of 1964—to come to the defense of South Vietnam, then near collapse under the weight of North Vietnam's aggression.

Clearly, then, there is something much deeper than simply your fear of death and destruction at work in preventing wars among democracies. This peacekeeping factor is analogous to what inhibits democratic nations from internal political violence. . . . Where democratic freedom flourishes in two countries, where there are free markets, and freedom of religion, association, ideas, and speech, then societies of mutual interest like corporations, partnerships, associations, societies, churches, schools, and clubs proliferate in and between the countries. Examples of these are the Catholic and Protestant Churches, Coca Cola, Disney, the Red Cross, the Boy Scouts, and the Association of Tennis Professionals. These cross-national groups become separate pyramids of power, competing with each other and with governments. As a result, both democratic nations then really comprise one society, one crosscut by these multifold groups, with multiple bonds between them.

Shared Interests

Moreover, between democratic governments there are many official and unofficial connections and linkages made to achieve similar functions and satisfy mutual interests. Their militaries freely coordinate strategies, and may even share equipment in line with their mutual defense arrangements and perceived common dangers. As example is nuclear weapons and military equipment shared by Great Britain and the United States. Intelligence services will share some secrets and even sometimes agents. Health services will coordinate their studies, undertake common projects, and provide health supplies when needed. Multiple shared and cross-pressured interests sew democratic societies together.

Politicians, leaders, and groups, therefore, have a common interest in keeping the peace. And where conflict might escalate into violence, as over some trade issue or fishing rights, interests are so cross-pressured by different groups and ties that the depth of feeling and single-minded devotion to the interest at stake is simply not there. Keep in mind that for democratic leaders to choose to make the huge jump to war against another country, there must be almost fanatical dedication to the interests—the stakes—involved, almost to the exclusion of all else.

A Common Culture

There is also something about democracies that is even more important than these links, bonds, and cross pressures. This is their democratic culture. Democratic peoples see one another as willing to compromise and negotiate issues rather than to fight violently over them. More important, they see one another as the same kind—part of one's in-group, one's moral universe. They each share not only socially, in overlapping groups, functions, and linkages, but also in political culture. Americans and Canadians, for example, have no expectation of fighting each other over trade restrictions and disputes. Both see each other as similarly free, democratic, and willing to bargain. And therefore, they have a totally unarmed 5,525-mile border between them. Similarly, with the development of a solid liberal democracy in Japan since the end of World War II, there is now no expectation of war between Japan and any other democracy, including the United States and democratic South Korea.

Finally, credit should be given to the ideology of democratic liberalism itself. Democratic liberals believe in the right of people to make their voices heard, to have a role in government, and to be free. Such liberals, who in domestic policy may be conservative, progressive, social democrat, Democrat, or Republican, greatly oppose any violence against other democracies. Even if those in power would consider such actions, democratic liberals—who compose the vast majority of intellectuals, journalists, and politicians—would arouse a storm of protest against them.

To summarize, there is no war between democracies because their people are free. This freedom creates a multitude of groups that produce diverse linkages across borders, cross-pressured interests, and make for an exchange culture of negotiation and compromise. Free people see each other as of the same kind, as morally similar, as negotiators instead of aggressors, and therefore have no expectation of war; and there is a prevalent ideology of democratic liberalism that believes in democratic freedom and opposes violence between democracies.

The Problems Facing Nondemocracies

Then why do nondemocracies—or rather, the dictators who control them, since by definition the people have little to say—make war on each other? Do not they see each other as of the same kind, sharing the same coercive culture? Yes, and that is exactly the problem for them. They live by coercion and force. Their guns keep them in power. They depend on a controlled populace manipulated through propaganda, deceit, and terror. Commands and decrees are the working routine of dictators; negotiations are a battleground in which one wins through lies, subterfuge, misinformation, stalling, and manipulation. A dictator's international relations are no different. They see them as war fought by other means. They will only truly negotiate in the face of bigger and and better guns, and they will only keep to their promises as long as these guns remain pointed at them. This is also how one dictator sees another—and, incidentally, how they see democracies.

This is not to say that war necessarily *will* happen between two countries if one or both is not democratic. They may be too far away from each other, too weak, or too inhibited by the greater power of a third country. It is only to say that the governments of such countries lack the social and cultural inhibitions that would prevent armed conflict between them, and that their dictatorial governments inherently encourage war. War may not happen, but it can, and the more undemocratic the governments, the more likely it will. . . .

The Magnitude of War

It is not just a free, democratic populace that inhibits war, but also the *degree* to which people are free. To understand this, you now have to stop thinking about war as a single event that happens or does not happen. Rather, think of war as embodying different amounts of killing, just as a yardstick embodies different degrees of length. A war may be as vast in scope as World War I or World War II, in which the fighting between Germany and the Soviet Union alone took more than 7,500,000 lives. But the severity of a war may only be in hundreds killed, not millions—as was the war between India and China in 1962, in which each lost around 500 dead, or the [1991 Persian] Gulf War [in which United Nations forces ejected Iraq from Kuwait], when the United

Figure 1. The Less Democratic Two Warring Regimes, the More Severe Their Wars 1900–1980

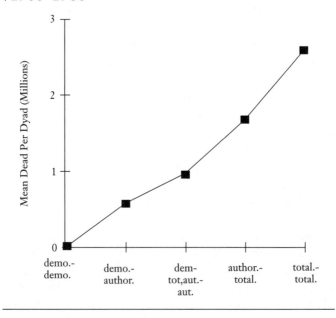

States lost 148 people from battle and 35 from friendly fire. All are wars, but the relevant distinction among them here is one of magnitude.

Then imagine a yardstick of freedom, where at one end you place democracies like Canada, New Zealand, and Sweden; and at the other end you put the least free countries, like North Korea, Sudan, Burma, Cuba, and Laos. Toward the middle would be such authoritarian countries as Egypt, Bangladesh, and Malaysia. Then for any two countries, the closer the government of each is to the democratic end of the yardstick, the more likely fewer will be killed in any war between them. Thus we can establish a correlation between the degree of freedom and the degree of intensity in war.

Figure 1 graphs this correlation for governments divided into democratic, authoritarian (people are partly free), and totalitarian (no freedom) subgroups. Then when measuring the international war dead between two governments, we find a near perfect correlation between freedom and war dead over the years 1900–1980. At one end of this correlation we have two nations that are both democratically (labeled "demo" in the figure) free and fought no wars and have, if any violence at all, very minor violence between the most marginal (electoral) democracies of them. At the other end, we have nations in which there are no civil rights and political liberties, and a dictator commands all politically relevant activity and groups. Such totalitarian governments (labeled "tot" or "total"), as the figure illustrates, are most likely to have the bloodiest wars. That part of World War II involving totalitarian Germany and the Soviet Union is a case in point. In fighting against each other, the Soviet Union lost 7,500,000 in battle, and Nazi Germany lost most of its 3,500,000 battle dead. No two nations have ever before or since inflicted such massive bloodshed on each other.

Authoritarian nations (labeled "aut" or "author") are between democratic and totalitarian ones in their degree of freedom; and, as should be true empirically, their violence is more or less, depending on whether it is with democracies or totalitarian nations.

To the iron law that democracies do not make war on each other, we can now add: The less democratically free any two

197

nations are, the more likely is severe violence between them.

There are many other kinds of international violence than war. There is violence short of war, such as American jets shooting down Iraqi fighter planes that violate the United Nations defined no-fly zone over southern Iraq; the blowing up of a South Korean passenger jet by North Korean agents; military action by Cuban forces against Somalia during the Ethiopia-Somalia War over the Ogaden (1976–1983). And despite this absence of violence *between* democracies, democracies overall could be as violent in international affairs as nondemocracies. *Democracies would just direct great violence at nondemocracies.*

Explaining Why Democracies Are Peaceful

However, when you consider the explanation for why democracies are peaceful—that democratic peoples are acculturated into negotiation and compromise over violence—you should expect that democracies overall would have the least severe foreign violence and war—the least dead in all their violence fighting other countries. Another way of putting this is that the more freedom a nation has, the less its leaders squander the lives of their people in foreign violence and war. . . . The facts are clear: The less democratic a country is, the more intense its foreign violence.

This is not to say that democracies are generally pacifist. They have engaged in bloody wars, usually to fight aggression and defend themselves and other democracies. And certainly democracies have also been the aggressors, as was the United States in the Spanish-American War, the Philippine-American War of 1899–1902, and the Grenada and Panama interventions. On the average, however, democratic leaders are more careful about the lives of their citizens and, therefore, they fight less severe wars.

There also are exceptions to this, as in the [World War I] Battle of the Somme during which the British commanding generals continued to throw troops into battle even after its bloody losses and lack of success. However, it should be pointed out again that the repercussions of this on British public opinion were so great as to make British foreign policy naively pacifist for a full generation. Totalitarian regimes have no such negative feedback. Their dictators can time after time, in war after war, use their people as mass instruments of war, like bullets and shells, throwing them at the enemy in human waves, for whatever purpose.

As a species, we have been killing ourselves by the millions in war after war throughout history. Now, finally, we have the power of knowledge to end forever, or at the very least drastically reduce, all this human slaughter. Freedom gives us the answer. Foster democratic freedom for all humanity to end this bloody scourge. And until we achieve this, foster at least some freedom where none exist to lessen the mass killing by war. War is an evil, and the fact that it has had to be fought by free people to preserve their freedom makes it no less so. What would eliminate this evil must be a moral good. And this is therefore another moral good of freedom.

"Threats . . . can be diminished through policies and programs designed to peacefully prevent the outbreak of violence and address the root causes of conflict."

Peaceful Intervention Can Prevent War

Friends Committee on National Legislation

The international community should work toward peaceful prevention strategies to eliminate the root causes of war, asserts the Friends Committee on National Legislation (FCNL) in the following viewpoint. Outdated tools such as unilateral military force are costly and only fuel threats, the authors contend. Instead of reacting to violence, they claim, nations worldwide should work together on peaceful prevention programs such as ending poverty, reducing weapons proliferation, advocating human rights, and averting public health crises. FCNL is a public interest lobby founded by the Religious Society of Friends—Quakers—who have a long history of peace activism.

As you read, consider the following questions:

1. According to FCNL, out of what did a new agenda for the peaceful prevention of armed conflict grow?
2. What did the United States do rather than apply the lessons of peaceful prevention, in the authors' view?
3. In FCNL's opinion, what did the New York City fire department do that could be applied to world conflict?

In the fall of 2002, the Bush Administration enshrined in U.S. policy a unilateral right to take military action against "emerging threats before they are fully formed." Months later, in March 2003, against widespread global protest and without United Nations Security Council authorization, the Administration put its new policy of "preemptive" war into practice by invading and occupying Iraq. The costs of the war, the path of fractured alliances left in its wake, the ongoing crisis with North Korea [over its weapons of mass destruction], and the growing realization that the war may have fueled the very threats it was intended to thwart, have demonstrated that the Bush Doctrine is far from a complete success in forging peace and security. In fact, military force and unilateralism are tragically ineffective instruments against the current threats facing the U.S. and the global community. But, if war is not the answer, then what is?

The Path to Lasting Security

The Bush Administration's focus on earlier response to emerging threats is an important and necessary step in U.S. policy. For too long, the world has responded too late to escalating conflicts, genocide, gross human rights abuses, failing states, the threat of terrorism, and the proliferation of weapons of mass destruction. Since the early 1990s, the international community has been facing up to and striving to overcome this "culture of reaction" by moving toward a "culture of prevention." Unfortunately, the Administration's emphasis on U.S. military and economic dominance and the use of force as its main instrument of foreign policy diverges drastically from the international community's deepened understanding of how to effectively reduce conflict and prevent war.

A growing body of research is contributing to a global movement for the peaceful prevention of deadly conflict. The publishing of the report of the Carnegie Commission on Preventing Deadly Conflict in 1998, followed three years later by the release of the Secretary-General's *Report on the Prevention of Armed Conflict* and the report *Responsibility to Protect* by the International Commission on Intervention and State Sovereignty marked important steps in the world community's effort to better understand, predict, and prevent the outbreak of violent conflict.

In 2001, [United Nations] Secretary-General Kofi Annan called for the development of new capacities within national governments, multilateral regional organizations, civil society, and the UN to undertake genuinely preventive actions in all stages of conflict—from latent tensions to hot wars to post-conflict peacebuilding. Such actions include developing early warning systems and enhanced preventive diplomacy capacities, strengthening international law and good governance, reducing the proliferation of weapons and protecting human rights, supporting sustainable development and the fair distribution of resources, ending poverty, tackling HIV/ AIDS and other public health crises, reducing ethnic tensions, building strong institutions of global civil society, and ensuring basic human security for all the world's people.

Policies of Peaceful Prevention

Many in the international community are already making progress to develop and implement policies of peaceful prevention. The European Union, African Union, and other multilateral organizations are working to develop new mechanisms for regional conflict prevention. Sweden has created a national policy for the prevention of violent conflict. The UN Development Program, World Bank, and national development agencies including the U.S. Agency for International Development (USAID) are exploring methods of integrating conflict prevention into their program work in countries worldwide. Non-governmental agencies across the globe working in humanitarian assistance, development, and peacebuilding have formed the Global Partnership for the Prevention of Armed Conflict, and are planning a conference to be held at the UN in 2005 that will help strengthen the role of civil society in conflict prevention.

A new agenda for the peaceful prevention of armed conflict originally grew out of the recognized failure of the international community in the post–Cold War world to adequately prevent mass humanitarian crises, including the Rwandan genocide and mass slaughter in Srebrenica. The international community, including the U.S., was growing tired of reacting too little, too late to humanitarian crises, ethnic conflicts, and state failures that might have been prevented. A paradigm shift away from 11th hour response to a model of early prevention was needed. In the summer of 2001, the UN Security Council, with the Bush Administration representing the U.S., passed a resolution pledging to "enhance the effectiveness of the United Nations in addressing conflict at all stages, from prevention to settlement to post-conflict peacebuilding." Secretary-General Kofi Annan urged the global community "to make prevention the cornerstone of collective security in the twenty-first century." In July 2003 the UN General Assembly adopted a landmark resolution in which Member States, including the U.S., committed to working towards the prevention of armed conflict, and laid out the roles of states, UN agencies, civil society and the private sector in preventing armed conflict.

The [terrorist] attacks of September 11, 2001 and ongoing threats of terrorism have highlighted the importance of implementing a security agenda that can better predict emerging threats, prevent their outbreak into violence, diffuse current disputes, and address the root causes of violent conflict. Rather than applying the lessons of peaceful prevention that the international community has been gathering, however, the U.S. has reverted to the outdated tools of unilateralism and overwhelming military force—instruments which promise to fuel the threats of weapons of mass destruction and terrorist attacks. Military action may stamp out some elements of a threat, but it cannot remove the roots of conflict and may instead deepen their reach.

A more effective, less costly path to national and global security is available.

Some years ago, the New York City fire department made a fundamental paradigm shift away from fire emergency response toward fire prevention. The department changed the way it approached its job and turned more energy and resources into public education, early detection systems, better building codes, and addressing some of the most persistent causes of fire. They saved lives and, over a few short years, began fighting fewer and less devastating fires. A similar shift in approach to conflict could save lives and reduce the occasion of war.

The U.S. can help lead this shift. The threats of weapons of mass destruction, terrorist networks, oppressive regimes, ethnic conflict, failed states, and devastating poverty and disease can be diminished through policies and programs designed to peacefully prevent the outbreak of violence and address the root causes of conflict. As U.S. Senator Joseph Biden (DE) proposed in late July 2003, "Instead of a preemption doctrine, what we need is a prevention doctrine which diffuses problems long before they explode in our face." Such a U.S. policy framework would build on the efforts already underway within some U.S. government agencies, at the UN, among European allies, in regional organizations, and among civil society groups to develop stronger capacities for early warning, early response, and addressing root causes. It would replace the policy of "preemptive" war with one of war prevention.

"Elimination of barriers to trade and the free intercourse among men would . . . reduce if not end the causes of war."

Promoting Individual Liberty and Free Trade Will Avoid War

Richard M. Ebeling

When nations abandon the ideals of individual freedom and free trade, wars cannot be avoided, argues Richard M. Ebeling in the following viewpoint. Interventionism—government involvement in other nations' affairs—and protectionism—government involvement in individual affairs—replace the ideals of liberty and economic freedom that prevent nations from choosing war. War can be avoided when people understand that the peaceful exchange of goods is preferable to plunder, and that others are persuaded to change by reason, not force. Ebeling, professor of economics at Hillsdale College in Michigan, is a scholar at the Ludwig von Mises Institute, which advocates individual freedom and free trade.

As you read, consider the following questions:
1. In Ebeling's view, why is war contrary to the long-run economic well-being of all belligerents?
2. According to the author, what happened once the spirit of economic freedom reached its zenith in the 1860s and 1870s?
3. What happened in Europe and Great Britain once war was declared in 1914, in the author's opinion?

Richard M. Ebeling, "Can Free Trade Really Prevent War?" delivered as part of a panel devoted to "The Warfare State," during the Ludwig von Mises Institute's Austrian Scholars Conference 8, March 15–16, 2002, in Auburn, Alabama. Reproduced by permission.

The Classical Liberals[1] of the nineteenth century were certain that the end of the old Mercantilist system—with its government control of trade and commerce, its bounties (subsidies) and prohibitions on exports and imports—would open wide vistas for improving the material conditions of man through the internationalization of the system of division of labor. They also believed that the elimination of barriers to trade and the free intercourse among men would help to significantly reduce if not end the causes of war among nations.

The economists of that earlier era had demonstrated the mutual gains from trade that would develop and be reinforced from specialization in productive activities among the people of the world. No longer would the material improvements of one nation be viewed as the inevitable cause of the poverty and economic hardships of other countries.

The Theory of Comparative Advantage

And with the addition of the theory of comparative advantage these economists were able show that even the "weak" and less productive in the world community could find a niche for their material betterment in the network of trade among nations. At the same time, the "strong" and more productive in that same community of nations would improve their circumstances by purchasing goods from the less productive so they could be freed to specialize in those lines of production in which they had a relative superiority.

Suppose that in the country of Superioristan, one yard of cloth can be produced in four hours and one bushel of potatoes can be harvested in one hour, while in the nation of Inferioristan, producing a yard of cloth takes twelve hours and harvesting a bushel of potatoes takes two hours. Clearly, Superioristan is a lower cost producer of both products in comparison to Inferioristan. Superioristan is three times more productive at cloth manufacturing and twice as productive in potato harvesting.

But equally clear is the fact that Superioristan is compar-

1. Classical Liberals, it is generally agreed, advocated the universal application of individual liberty, free trade, and limited government.

atively more cost-efficient in cloth manufacturing. That is, when Superioristan foregoes the manufacture of a yard of cloth, it can harvest four bushels of potatoes. But when Inferioristan foregoes the manufacture of a yard of cloth, it can harvest six bushels of potatoes. If Superioristan and Inferioristan were to exchange cloth for potatoes at the price ratio of, say, one yard of cloth for five bushels of potatoes, both nations could be made better off, with Superioristan specializing in cloth manufacturing and Inferioristan in potato harvesting. Superioristan would now receive five bushels of potatoes for a yard of its cloth, rather than the four bushels if it harvested at home all the potatoes it consumed. And Inferioristan would receive a yard of cloth for only giving up five bushels of potatoes, rather than the six bushels if it manufactured at home all of the cloth it used.

Thus, in the middle of the eighteenth century, [historian and philosopher] David Hume could declare, in his famous essay, "Of the Jealousy of Trade," "I shall therefore venture to acknowledge that, not only as a man, but as a British subject, I pray for the flourishing commerce of Germany, Spain, Italy, and even France itself." The wealthier and more productive a nation's potential trading partners, the greater the number and the less expensive the array of goods that it may be able to obtain through exchange in comparison to being solely dependent for its material well-being upon its own domestic productive capabilities.

A Grander Vision

But the Classical Liberals believed that free trade meant more than just a more plentiful supply of goods and services. They also were confident that with freedom of trade would come a world of peace and international tranquility. As the French economist, Frederic Passy, expressed it in the 1840s,

> Some day all barriers will fall; some day mankind, constantly united by continuous transactions, will form just one workshop, one market, and one family. . . . And this is . . . the grandeur, the truth, the nobility, I might almost say the holiness of the free-trade doctrine; by the prosaic but effective pressure of [material] interest it tends to make justice and harmony prevail in the world.

War, therefore, is not only destructive but also contrary to the long-run economic well-being of all belligerents because it disrupts the existing or potential bonds of the division of labor from which the prosperity can come to replace the poverty and conflicts of mankind. "War," Frederic Passy declared, "is no longer merely a crime; it is an absurdity. It is no longer merely immoral and cruel; it is stupid. It is no longer merely murder on a large scale; it is suicide and voluntary ruin."

The nineteenth century was not without war and international conflict. But in comparison to earlier centuries, and certainly in comparison to the twentieth century, the hundred years between the defeat of Napoleon [Bonaparte, French emperor] in 1815 and the opening shots of the First World War in 1914 was a period of relative peace and international attempts to devise "rules of warfare." If war continued to happen, then it should be controlled and limited in its destructive effect on life and property, especially of the innocent noncombatants of the belligerent countries and the citizens of neutral nations. There were a wide variety of international conferences and treaties in the nineteenth and first decade of the twentieth centuries that specified these rules of war on land and sea and in the air (the treaties delineated what was and what was not permissible with the use of balloons in combat).

A Century of War

All of the treaties and agreements and all of the hopes that international trade would establish a web of mutual interdependency in the areas of commerce, culture, and communication, which would make war impossible or at least more "civilized," died on the battlefields of Europe in 1914. Economic nationalism then joined political collectivism in the two decades before the two World Wars. And the Second World War threw to the winds all restraints on the conduct of nations, as unrestricted methods of warfare were joined by mass murder and the barbaric brutalizing of tens of millions of innocent and unarmed men, women, and children.

The half century following World War II witnessed wars, civil wars, and massacres of millions, once again, in Asia and

Africa with the end of European colonialism on those continents. And for this entire period the world was split in two by the ideological and military rivalry of the United States and the Soviet Union. As a result, the United States fought two major wars, in Korea and Vietnam. The Soviet's violently repressed opposition and revolts in East Germany, Hungary, and Czechoslovakia, and fought a ten-year war in Afghanistan.

The People Want Peace

I like to believe that people in the long run are going to do more to promote peace than our governments. Indeed, I think that people want peace so much that one of these days governments had better get out of their way and let them have it.

Dwight D. Eisenhower, TV talk with British prime minister Maurice Macmillan, August 31, 1959.

In the post-Soviet era, and in spite of the end of the cold war, wars have continued around the world, including the Persian Gulf War in 1991, the disintegration of Yugoslavia and foreign intervention in Bosnia and Kosovo. And now, following the terrorist attacks in New York and Washington, D.C., in September 2001, the United States has attacked and militarily overthrown the government of Afghanistan and threatened war against an "axis of evil" comprised of Iraq, Iran, and North Korea.

Abandoning Freedom

None of the wars, conflicts, and mass murders of the twentieth century can be blamed on free trade or explained in terms of free trade. The entire last one hundred years was a revolt against the ideas and ideals of the Classical Liberals of the nineteenth century. When the United States and Great Britain at the end of the Second World War stated their intention of establishing a new economic order for the world, their goal and the institutions arising from their intention was for international managed trade, not global free trade. [Austrian economist and philosopher] Ludwig von Mises observed during the Second World War that

A nation's policy forms an integral whole. Foreign policy and domestic policy are closely linked together, they condition each other. Economic nationalism is the corollary of the present-day domestic policies of government interference with business and of national planning as free trade was the complement of domestic economic freedom.

The interventionist and planning ideas during the last one hundred years meant that trade among nations could not be left outside of government oversight and control, lest the directions and patterns of international trade undermine and frustrate the goals and purposes of national governments in their domestic affairs.

Free trade was unable to prevent war in the twentieth century because by 1914, very few people believed any longer in the idea of liberty. The spirit of economic freedom reached its zenith in the 1860s and 1870s. From then on a counter-revolution began against freedom. Germany was a major catalyst for the change in ideological and policy direction with its return to protectionism and implementation of many programs of the modern welfare state. But France also started to move in this direction with regulations and pressures that gave the government increasing influence and, in fact, control over the patterns of French foreign investment in other countries to reinforce its political foreign policy objectives, as well as restrictions on foreign investments made inside France. And even in Great Britain, which retained the closest approximation to free trade principles for the longest time—until the opening shots of the First World War—the London investment houses would informally make sure that their foreign loans and investments did not conflict with the wider policy goals of the British government. The First World War was the culmination of this process, with nation and state completely becoming one as belligerent powers made all aspects of social and economic life subservient to the ends of war.

The Rise of Interventionism and Protectionism

In the aftermath of that war, Ludwig von Mises explained in 1924 that no institution for peaceful cooperation is secure if the ideological currents shift and public policy becomes dominated by the spirit of interventionism and war:

> Only one thing can conquer war—the liberal attitude of mind which can see nothing in war but destruction and annihilation, and which can never wish to bring about a war, because it regards war as injurious even to the victors. Where Liberalism prevails, there will never be war. But where there are other opinions concerning the profitability and injuriousness of war, no rules or regulations, however cunningly devised, can make war impossible.

The context in which Mises made this remark was whether or not a full, one-hundred-percent gold-coin monetary system would have been able to withstand the trend toward war, if government needed control of the monetary system to fund its war expenditures.

> If war is regarded as advantageous, then laws regulating the monetary systems will not be allowed to stand in the way of going to war. On the first day of any war, all the laws opposing obstacles to it will be swept away, just as in 1914 the monetary legislation of all the belligerent States was turned upside down without one word of protest being ventured.

Nor would have a completely free banking system, totally outside the control of the government, fared any better in 1914, Mises believed.

> The answer to this question seems to be that it would not have done so. The governments of the belligerent—and neutral—States overthrew the whole system of bank legislation with a stroke of a pen, and they could have done so just the same if the banks had been uncontrolled.

The Winds of War

Great Britain, in spite of the growing protectionism and interventionism in other European countries in the years leading up to 1914, had followed an open, free-trade policy throughout its Empire. There had been free movement of goods and free movement of men, the latter without either passports or visas. And capital moved without restriction both into and out of Great Britain itself and throughout the far reaches of the Empire. Yet overnight barriers and restrictions went up all across the European continent, including in Britain, once war was declared and the opening volleys were fired. Almost seventy years of British free trade, with all of its benefits, were brought to an end with a few strokes of the pen of war emergency acts.

Mises did not discount the significance of institutional barriers to arbitrary government actions. He pointed out that, indeed, if the countries of Europe in 1914 had still had gold standards fully based on gold coins in circulation, to which the people were accustomed and which in their minds symbolized the security and soundness of the monetary system, governments may very will have had a harder time justifying the abolition of the monetary order and the resort to inflation to finance their war expenditures. "It would not be so easy for governments to disavow the reactions of war on the monetary system; they will be obliged to justify their policy."

But neither the gold standard as practiced in 1914 nor international freedom of trade as existing in 1914 could withstand the winds of war. The "spirit of the times" had long before changed from a belief in individual freedom, limited government, and free markets with the accompanying depoliticizing of interpersonal relationships, including in matters of international commerce and investment, into a reborn desire for protectionism, nationalism, planning, and imperialism.

The Prerequisites of Peace

Free trade cannot prevent war when men no longer believe in peace. Free trade is premised on the idea that human relationships should be voluntary and based on mutual consent. It is grounded on the understanding that the material, cultural, and spiritual improvements in the circumstances and conditions of man are best served when the members of the global community of mankind specialize their activities in a world-encompassing social system of division of labor. It requires the conviction that the moral condition of individual men and mankind as a whole is fostered the most when people acquire the things of the world that they desire by peaceful exchange rather than by theft and plunder; and when men attempt to change the way their fellow human beings think and live and act by using the methods of reason, persuasion, and example instead of through the use of compulsion, power, terror, and death.

That is why wars still plague us. Too many men still don't believe in peace because they don't believe in the prerequisites for peace and the freedom of trade that accompanies their implementation. Just as the Second World War was about to begin, the French free-market economist, Louis Boudin, pointed out,

> The system of non-regulated international trade cannot ensure peace. It can help to create a peaceful atmosphere, on the one condition: that men have a peaceful mental attitude. . . . Peace within a nation requires the same condition. . . . The essential task therefore is *to create a peaceful mentality.*

The task we face today is still the same as when Ludwig von Mises wrote the words quoted above in 1924 and Boudin penned his words in 1939. We must continue to fight and hopefully prevail through reason and argument against what [economist] Adam Smith referred to in 1776 as the "prejudices of the public" (the economic ignorance of our fellow men) and the opposition of the "private interests" (those who wish to use the power of the state to plunder others in society). Until we do, free trade will not replace and then help to prevent future wars.

"Although war is a great evil, it does have a great virtue: it can resolve political conflicts and lead to peace."

Letting Wars Run Their Course Leads to Lasting Peace

Edward N. Luttwak

In the following viewpoint Edward N. Luttwak argues that international peacekeeping and humanitarian efforts do not prevent war. In fact, he claims, such policies interrupt the natural course of wars and needlessly prolong them. If the United Nations and international organizations let all wars run their course, he contends, lasting peace between nations will result. Luttwak is a senior fellow at the Center for Strategic and International Studies, a foreign policy think tank.

As you read, consider the following questions:
1. In Luttwak's opinion, how have the consequences of cease-fires increased now that the Cold War is over?
2. Why is appeasing the locally stronger force not strategically purposeful, in the author's view?
3. According to the author, how are postwar camps in Europe different from those in Lebanon, Syria, Jordan, the West Bank, and the Gaza Strip?

Edward N. Luttwak, "Give War a Chance," *Foreign Affairs*, vol. 78, July/August 1999. Copyright © 1999 by the Council on Foreign Relations, Inc. Reproduced by permission.

An unpleasant truth often overlooked is that although war is a great evil, it does have a great virtue: it can resolve political conflicts and lead to peace. This can happen when all belligerents become exhausted or when one wins decisively. Either way the key is that the fighting must continue until a resolution is reached. War brings peace only after passing a culminating phase of violence. Hopes of military success must fade for accommodation to become more attractive than further combat.

War Interrupted

Since the establishment of the United Nations and the enshrinement of great-power politics in its Security Council, however, wars among lesser powers have rarely been allowed to run their natural course. Instead, they have typically been interrupted early on, before they could burn themselves out and establish the preconditions for a lasting settlement. Cease-fires and armistices have frequently been imposed under the aegis of the Security Council in order to halt fighting. NATO's [North Atlantic Treaty Organization's] intervention in the Kosovo crisis follows this pattern.

But a cease-fire tends to arrest war-induced exhaustion and lets belligerents reconstitute and rearm their forces. It intensifies and prolongs the struggle once the cease-fire ends—and it does usually end. This was true of the Arab-Israeli war of 1948–49, which might have come to closure in a matter of weeks if two cease-fires ordained by the Security Council had not let the combatants recuperate. It has recently been true in the Balkans. Imposed cease-fires frequently interrupted the fighting between Serbs and Croats in Krajina, between the forces of the rump Yugoslav federation and the Croat army, and between the Serbs, Croats, and Muslims in Bosnia. Each time, the opponents used the pause to recruit, train, and equip additional forces for further combat, prolonging the war and widening the scope of its killing and destruction. Imposed armistices, meanwhile—again, unless followed by negotiated peace accords—artificially freeze conflict and perpetuate a state of war indefinitely by shielding the weaker side from the consequences of refusing to make concessions for peace.

Post–Cold War Cease-Fires

The Cold War provided compelling justification for such behavior by the two superpowers, which sometimes collaborated in coercing less-powerful belligerents to avoid being drawn into their conflicts and clashing directly. Although imposed cease-fires ultimately did increase the total quantity of warfare among the lesser powers, and armistices did perpetuate states of war, both outcomes were clearly lesser evils (from a global point of view) than the possibility of nuclear war. But today, neither Americans nor Russians are inclined to intervene competitively in the wars of lesser powers, so the unfortunate consequences of interrupting war persist while no greater danger is averted. It might be best for all parties to let minor wars burn themselves out.

Today cease-fires and armistices are imposed on lesser powers by multilateral agreement—not to avoid great-power competition but for essentially disinterested and indeed frivolous motives, such as television audiences' revulsion at harrowing scenes of war. But this, perversely, can systematically prevent the transformation of war into peace. The Dayton accords are typical of the genre: they have condemned Bosnia to remain divided into three rival armed camps, with combat suspended momentarily but a state of hostility prolonged indefinitely. Since no side is threatened by defeat and loss, none has a sufficient incentive to negotiate a lasting settlement; because no path to peace is even visible, the dominant priority is to prepare for future war rather than to reconstruct devastated economies and ravaged societies. Uninterrupted war would certainly have caused further suffering and led to an unjust outcome from one perspective or another, but it would also have led to a more stable situation that would have let the postwar era truly begin. Peace takes hold only when war is truly over.

The Problems of Peacekeepers

A variety of multilateral organizations now make it their business to intervene in other peoples' wars. The defining characteristic of these entities is that they insert themselves in war situations while refusing to engage in combat. In the long run this only adds to the damage. If the United Nations helped the strong defeat the weak faster and more decisively, it would actually enhance the peacemaking potential of war. But the first priority of U.N. peacekeeping contingents is to avoid casualties among their own personnel. Unit commanders therefore habitually appease the locally stronger force, accepting its dictates and tolerating its abuses. This appeasement is not strategically purposeful, as siding with the stronger power overall would be; rather, it merely reflects the determination of each U.N. unit to avoid confrontation. The final result is to prevent the emergence of a coherent outcome, which requires an imbalance of strength sufficient to end the fighting.

Branch. © 1999 by *San Antonio Express News*. Reproduced by permission.

Peacekeepers chary of violence are also unable to effectively protect civilians who are caught up in the fighting or deliberately attacked. At best, U.N. peacekeeping forces have been passive spectators to outrages and massacres, as in Bosnia and Rwanda; at worst, they collaborate with it, as Dutch U.N. troops did in the fall of Srebenica by helping the Bosnian Serbs separate the men of military age from the rest of the population.

The very presence of U.N. forces, meanwhile, inhibits the normal remedy of endangered civilians, which is to escape from the combat zone. Deluded into thinking that they will be protected, civilians in danger remain in place until it is too late to flee. During the 1992–94 siege of Sarajevo, appeasement interacted with the pretense of protection in an especially perverse manner: U.N. personnel inspected outgoing flights to prevent the escape of Sarajevo civilians in obedience to a cease-fire agreement negotiated with the locally dominant Bosnian Serbs—who habitually violated that deal. The more sensible, realistic response to a raging war would have been for the Muslims to either flee the city or drive the Serbs out.

Limited Effectiveness

Institutions such as the European Union, the Western European Union, and the Organization for Security and Cooperation in Europe lack even the U.N.'s rudimentary command structure and personnel, yet they too now seek to intervene in warlike situations, with predictable consequences. Bereft of forces even theoretically capable of combat, they satisfy the interventionist urges of member states (or their own institutional ambitions) by sending unarmed or lightly armed "observer" missions, which have the same problems as U.N. peacekeeping missions, only more so.

Military organizations such as NATO or the West African Peacekeeping Force (ECOMOG, recently at work in Sierra Leone) are capable of stopping warfare. Their interventions still have the destructive consequence of prolonging the state of war, but they can at least protect civilians from its consequences. Even that often fails to happen, however, because multinational military commands engaged in disinterested interventions tend to avoid any risk of combat, thereby limiting their effectiveness. U.S. troops in Bosnia, for example, repeatedly failed to arrest known war criminals passing through their checkpoints lest this provoke confrontation.

Multinational commands, moreover, find it difficult to control the quality and conduct of member states' troops, which can reduce the performance of all forces involved to the lowest common denominator. This was true of otherwise fine British troops in Bosnia and of the Nigerian marines in Sierra Leone. The phenomenon of troop degradation can rarely be detected by external observers, although its consequences are abundantly visible in the litter of dead, mutilated, raped, and tortured victims that attends such interventions. The true state of affairs is illuminated by the rare exception, such as the vigorous Danish tank battalion in Bosnia that replied to any attack on it by firing back in full force, quickly stopping the fighting. . . .

Creating Refugee Nations

The most disinterested of all interventions in war—and the most destructive—are humanitarian relief activities. The largest and most protracted is the United Nations Relief and Works Agency (UNRWA). It was built on the model of its predecessor, the United Nations Relief and Rehabilitation Agency (UNRRA), which operated displaced-persons' camps in Europe immediately after World War II. The UNRWA was established immediately after the 1948–49 Arab-Israeli war to feed, shelter, educate, and provide health services for Arab refugees who had fled Israeli zones in the former territory of Palestine.

By keeping refugees alive in spartan conditions that encouraged their rapid emigration or local resettlement, the UNRRA's camps in Europe had assuaged postwar resentments and helped disperse revanchist concentrations of national groups. But UNRWA camps in Lebanon, Syria, Jordan, the West Bank, and the Gaza Strip provided on the whole a higher standard of living than most Arab villagers had previously enjoyed, with a more varied diet, organized schooling, superior medical care, and no backbreaking labor in stony fields. They had, therefore, the opposite effect, becoming desirable homes rather than eagerly abandoned transit camps. With the encouragement of several Arab countries, the UNRWA turned escaping civilians into lifelong refugees who gave birth to refugee children, who have in turn had refugee children of their own.

During its half-century of operation, the UNRWA has thus perpetuated a Palestinian refugee nation, preserving its resentments in as fresh a condition as they were in 1948 and keeping the first bloom of revanchist emotion intact. By its very existence, the UNRWA dissuades integration into local society and inhibits emigration. The concentration of Palestinians in the camps, moreover, has facilitated the voluntary or forced enlistment of refugee youths by armed organizations that fight both Israel and each other. The UNRWA has contributed to a half-century of Arab-Israeli violence and still retards the advent of peace.

If each European war had been attended by its own post-war UNRWA, today's Europe would be filled with giant camps for millions of descendants of uprooted Gallo-Romans, abandoned Vandals, defeated Burgundians, and misplaced Visigoths—not to speak of more recent refugee nations such as post-1945 Sudeten Germans (three million of whom were expelled from Czechoslovakia in 1945). Such a Europe would have remained a mosaic of warring tribes, undigested and unreconciled in their separate feeding camps. It might have assuaged consciences to help each one at each remove, but it would have led to permanent instability and violence.

The UNRWA has counterparts elsewhere, such as the Cambodian camps along the Thai border, which incidentally provided safe havens for the mass-murdering Khmer Rouge. But because the United Nations is limited by stingy national contributions, these camps' sabotage of peace is at least localized.

Nongovernmental Interference

That is not true of the proliferating, feverishly competitive nongovernmental organizations (NGOs) that now aid war refugees. Like any other institution, these NGOs are interested in perpetuating themselves, which means that their first priority is to attract charitable contributions by being seen to be active in high-visibility situations. Only the most dramatic natural disasters attract any significant mass-media attention, and then only briefly; soon after an earthquake or flood, the cameras depart. War refugees, by contrast, can win sustained press coverage if kept concentrated in reasonably accessible camps. Regular warfare among well-developed countries is rare and offers few opportunities for such NGOs, so they focus their efforts on aiding refugees in the poorest parts of the world. This ensures that the food, shelter, and health care offered—although abysmal by Western standards—exceeds what is locally available to non-refugees. The consequences are entirely predictable. Among many examples, the huge refugee camps along the Democratic Republic of Congo's border with Rwanda stand out. They sustain a Hutu nation that would otherwise have been dispersed, making the consolidation of Rwanda impossible and providing a base for radicals to launch more Tutsi-killing raids across the border. Humanitarian intervention has worsened the chances of a stable, long-term resolution of the tensions in Rwanda.

To keep refugee nations intact and preserve their resentments forever is bad enough, but inserting material aid into ongoing conflicts is even worse. Many NGOs that operate in an odor of sanctity routinely supply active combatants. Defenseless, they cannot exclude armed warriors from their feeding stations, clinics, and shelters. Since refugees are presumptively on the losing side, the warriors among them are usually in retreat. By intervening to help, NGOs systematically impede the progress of their enemies toward a decisive victory that could end the war. Sometimes NGOs, impartial to a fault, even help both sides, thus preventing mutual exhaustion and a resulting settlement. And in some extreme cases, such as Somalia, NGOs even pay protection money to local war bands, which use those funds to buy arms. Those NGOs are therefore helping prolong the warfare whose consequences they ostensibly seek to mitigate.

Too many wars nowadays become endemic conflicts that never end because the transformative effects of both decisive victory and exhaustion are blocked by outside intervention. Unlike the ancient problem of war, however, the compounding of its evils by disinterested interventions is a new malpractice that could be curtailed. Policy elites should actively resist the emotional impulse to intervene in other peoples' wars—not because they are indifferent to human suffering but precisely because they care about it and want to facilitate the advent of peace. The United States should dissuade multilateral interventions instead of leading them. New rules should be established for U.N. refugee relief activities to ensure that immediate succor is swiftly followed by repatriation, local absorption, or emigration, ruling out the establishment of permanent refugee camps. And although it may not be possible to constrain interventionist NGOs, they should at least be neither officially encouraged nor funded. Underlying these seemingly perverse measures would be a true appreciation of war's paradoxical logic and a commitment to let it serve its sole useful function: to bring peace.

Periodical Bibliography

The following articles have been selected to supplement the
diverse views presented in this chapter.

Steven Brion-Meisels
and Glen Stassen
"If War Is Not the Answer, What Is?"
Cambridge Chronicle, September 10, 2003.

James Carroll
"We Must All Prevent War," *Boston Globe*, May
28, 2002.

Priscilla Elworthy
"Bomb-Catching," *New Internationalist*,
September 2003.

Priscilla Elworthy
"War Prevention Works: Conflict Resolution
in the 21st Century," *Hope Dance*, June/July
2002.

Peter J. Gomes
"'Patriotism Is Not Enough'; Christian
Conscience in Time of War," *Sojourners*,
January/February 2003.

Anne Goodman
"Cultures of Peace, the Hidden Side of
History," *Peace Magazine*, January–March 2001.

Tenzin Gyatso
"Peace: Truth, Justice, and Freedom," *Vital
Speeches of the Day*, November 15, 2001.

Kim Dae Jung
"Closing the Digital Gap Is Key to Peace,"
New Perspectives Quarterly, Spring 2002.

Gabriel Moran
"Outlawing War: Reforming the Language of
War Is the First Step Toward Ending It,"
National Catholic Reporter, November 7, 2003.

Hanna Newcombe
"Uses of Democracy," *Peace Magazine*,
January–March 2001.

Jonathan Power
"War Can Be Prevented," *Jordan Times*,
October 30, 2003.

Michael Renner
"How to Abolish War," *Humanist*, July 1999.

Sebastian Rosato
"The Flawed Logic of Democratic Peace
Theory," *American Political Science Review*,
November 2003.

Frank A. Thomas
"Love That Conquers Fear," *Other Side*,
January/February 2003.

Peter Weiss
"Nuclear Weapons and Preventive War," *Global
Policy Forum*, November 2, 2003.

Michael Welsch
"Patriotism Is Not the Highest Calling,"
National Catholic Reporter, April 18, 2003.

For Further Discussion

Chapter 1

1. Daniel C. Tosteson claims that as technology brings people closer, clashes over conflicting religious beliefs increase. Vincent Carroll asserts that such claims are exaggerated. He contends that what some believe to be wars over conflicting religious beliefs are actually secular conflicts over power and resources. These authors have significantly different attitudes toward religion. How is each author's attitude toward religion reflected in his argument? Explain, citing from both viewpoints.

2. Steven Staples contends that globalization creates economic inequity and competition for diminishing resources, which he believes are the root causes of war. Daniel T. Griswold, on the other hand, argues that globalization increases income and education levels, which in turn promote political and civil liberty, conditions that he maintains reduce the likelihood of war. Although the authors differ in their attitude toward globalization, what similarities do you find in their explanation of the root causes of war? Citing their viewpoints, explain.

3. While the Green Party of Great Britain believes that the competition that capitalism inspires leads to war, Andrew Bernstein contends that capitalist competition creates the economic freedom and prosperity that lead to peace. Of the two authors, which do you think provides the most convincing evidence? Explain, citing from the viewpoints.

4. Several of the authors in this chapter have identified what they believe are the causes of war. Which cause(s), if addressed, do you think would reduce the likelihood of war? Explain.

Chapter 2

1. George Weigel argues that when dealing with terrorists and rogue states, violence is sometimes necessary to maintain peace and freedom. Wendell Berry claims that violence can never prevent further violence. Which of the following scenarios do you think would prevent escalating violence: choosing to fight a bully or refusing to fight and facing the possibility of ridicule and/or physical abuse? Is it possible to apply this question to international affairs when the decision to fight or not to fight involves innocent civilians? Explain.

2. Charles W. Kegley Jr. and Gregory A. Raymond maintain that expanding the just war doctrine to allow preemptive attacks en-

courages nations to begin wars indiscriminately based on spurious claims of self-defense. Michael J. Glennon provides several examples in his viewpoint to support his contention that preemptive war is justified to deter future attacks. Which of Glennon's examples, if any, do you think Kegley and Raymond would agree justifies a preemptive strike in self-defense? Explain, citing from the viewpoints.

3. The Institute for American Values asserts that the war on terrorism is justified to protect innocents from terrorist attacks. Tim Wise claims, however, that the war on terrorism does not prevent terrorism. In fact, the war itself takes innocent lives, he argues. Wise maintains that those who argue in favor of the war on terrorism have confused the concepts of naïveté and realism. Citing from the viewpoints, which author do you believe is being naive and which realistic?

Chapter 3

1. Bruce Shapiro argues that detainees in the war on terror should be treated as prisoners of war and thus protected by the Geneva Conventions so that U.S. soldiers will be treated accordingly. Ronald D. Rotunda maintains that treating detainees suspected of terrorism as prisoners of war will not change the way terrorists treat our soldiers or our citizens. Do you believe terrorists and the regimes that support them will be influenced by how the United States treats detainees in the war on terror? Explain.

2. The deliberate targeting of civilians is an act of terrorism and cannot be justified by the desire to spare one's own soldiers, Brian Carnell claims. Onkar Ghate contends, on the other hand, that to win wars against aggression, civilians must be sacrificed. Carnell sees civilians as innocent while Ghate does not. Do you think civilians are "innocent"? Explain, citing from the viewpoints.

3. Michael Byers and Jonathan F. Fanton agree that because of its position as a world leader and its military might, the United States should abide by international laws of war that place a high value on humanitarian concerns. David B. Rivkin, Lee A. Casey, and Ruth Wedgwood disagree, arguing that these laws limit America's ability to conduct war and make it vulnerable to accusations of war crimes. Which view do you find more persuasive? Explain, citing from the viewpoints.

Chapter 4

1. Victor Davis Hanson argues that war is inevitable. The only way to prevent war, he claims, is by maintaining a strong military. Is

Hanson's war-prevention strategy dependent on the premise that war is inevitable? Explain.

2. R.J. Rummel maintains that democracies do not fight each other and thus increasing democracy worldwide should reduce war. In supporting his position that promoting both individual liberty and free trade will prevent war, Richard M. Ebeling argues that imposing democratic ideals by force promotes, rather than prevents war. If both authors are correct, what efforts to increase democracy worldwide do you believe will be more likely to further the cause of peace? Explain, citing real-world or hypothetical examples.

3. Edward N. Luttwak argues that interference in wars merely prolongs them, and wars must run their course in order to achieve lasting peace. Do you think it likely that most developed nations will stand by and let all wars run their course? Explain, citing real-world examples.

4. The authors in this chapter suggest several ways that war might be prevented. Which do you find most persuasive? Explain.

Organizations to Contact

The editors have compiled the following list of organizations concerned with the issues debated in this book. The descriptions are derived from materials provided by the organizations. All have publications or information available for interested readers. The list was compiled on the date of publication of the present volume; the information provided here may change. Be aware that many organizations take several weeks or longer to respond to inquiries, so allow as much time as possible.

Amnesty International USA
322 Eighth Ave., New York, NY 10001
(212) 807-8400 • fax: (212) 627-1451
Web site: www.amnesty-usa.org

Amnesty International works to ensure that governments do not deny individuals their basic human rights as outlined in the United Nations Universal Declaration of Human Rights. It publishes numerous books, the quarterly magazine *Amnesty Now*, an annual report, and reports on individual countries. Its Web site contains recent news, reports, and a searchable database of archived publications.

Brookings Institution
1775 Massachusetts Ave. NW, Washington, DC 20036
(202) 797-6000 • fax: (202) 797-6004
e-mail: brookinfo@brook.edu • Web site: www.brook.edu

Founded in 1927, the institution conducts research and analyzes global events and their impact on the United States and U.S. foreign policy. It publishes the quarterly *Brookings Review* and numerous books and research papers on foreign policy. Its Web site publishes editorials, papers, testimony, reports, and articles written by Brookings' scholars, including "War, Profits, and the Vacuum of Law: Privatized Military Firms and International Law" and "An Alliance of Democracies."

Cato Institute
1000 Massachusetts Ave. NW, Washington, DC 20001-5403
(202) 842-0200 • fax: (202) 842-3490
Web site: www.cato.org

Cato is a libertarian public policy research foundation dedicated to peace and limited government intervention in foreign affairs. It publishes numerous reports and periodicals, including *Policy Analysis* and *Cato Policy Review*, both of which discuss U.S. policy in regional conflicts. Its Web site contains a searchable database of institute articles, news, and commentary, including "Congress and the Power of War and Peace" and "The Wages of War."

Center for Strategic and International Studies (CSIS)
1800 K St. NW, Washington, DC 20006
(202) 887-0200 • fax: (202) 775-3199
Web site: www.csis.org

CSIS is a public policy research institution that specializes in the areas of U.S. domestic and foreign policy, national security, and economic policy. The center analyzes world crises and recommends U.S. military and defense polities. Its publications report on issues of interest to the center. Its Web site has a searchable database of news, articles, testimony, and reports, including "Winning the War on Terror" and "The 'Post Conflict' Lessons of Iraq and Afghanistan."

Coalition for the International Criminal Court (CICC)
c/o WFM, 777 UN Plaza, New York, NY 10017
(212) 687-2176 • fax: (212) 599-1332
e-mail: cicc@iccnow.org • Web site: www.iccnow.org

CICC is a network of over two thousand nongovernmental organizations advocating for a fair, effective, and independent International Criminal Court (ICC). CICC publishes the semiannual *ICC Monitor*, recent issues of which are available on its Web site. The CICC Web site also publishes fact sheets and statements in support of the ICC.

Council on Foreign Relations
58 E. Sixty-eighth St., New York, NY 10021
(212) 434-9400 • fax: (212) 434-9800
Web site: www.cfr.org

The council specializes in foreign affairs and studies the international aspects of American political and economic policies and problems. Its journal *Foreign Affairs*, published five times a year, includes analyses of current conflicts around the world. Its Web site publishes editorials, interviews, and articles, including "The Humanitarian Transformation: Expanding Global Intervention Capacity" and "Is World Peace Through Conflict Prevention Possible?"

Crimes of War Project
1205 Lamont St. NW, Washington, DC 20010
(202) 494-3834 • fax: (202) 387-6858
e-mail: office@crimesofwar.org • Web site: www.crimesofwar.org

The Crimes of War Project is a collaboration of journalists, lawyers, and scholars dedicated to raising public awareness of the laws of war. The project publishes *Crimes of War* magazine, recent issues of which are available on its Web site. The Web site also makes available essays and reports, including "Israel and the Palestinians: What Laws Were Broken?" and "Iraq and the 'Bush Doctrine' of Pre-Emptive Self-Defense."

Foreign Policy Association (FPA)
470 Park Ave. South, 2nd Fl., New York, NY 10016
(212) 481-8100 • fax: (212) 481-9275
e-mail: info@fpa.org • Web site: www.fpa.org

FPA is a nonprofit organization that believes a concerned and informed public is the foundation for an effective foreign policy. Publications such as the annual *Great Decisions* briefing book and the newsletters *FPA Today* and *Global Views* cover foreign policy issues worldwide. Its Web site has an extensive searchable resource library of articles, reports, and speeches.

Global Exchange
2017 Mission, #303, San Francisco, CA 94110
(415) 255-7296 • fax: (415) 255-7498
e-mail: info@globalexchange.org
Web site: www.globalexchange.org

Global Exchange is a human rights organization that exposes economic and political injustice around the world. In response to such injustices, the organization supports education, activism, and a noninterventionist U.S. foreign policy. It publishes the quarterly newsletter *Global Exchange.*

Heritage Foundation
214 Massachusetts Ave. NE, Washington, DC 20002-4999
(202) 546-4400 • fax: (202) 546-8328
e-mail: pubs@heritage.org • Web site: www.heritage.org

The foundation is a public policy research institute that advocates limited government and the free-market system. The foundation publishes the quarterly *Policy Review* as well as monographs, books, and papers supporting U.S. noninterventionism. Its Web site contains news and commentary and searchable databases.

Human Rights Watch
350 Fifth Ave., 34th Fl., New York, NY 10118-3299
(212) 290-4700 • fax: (212) 736-1300
e-mail: hrwnyc@hrw.org • Web site: www.hrw.org

Founded in 1978, this nongovernmental organization conducts systematic investigations of human rights abuses in countries around the world. It publishes many books and reports on specific countries and issues as well as annual reports, recent selections of which are available on its Web site.

International Committee of the Red Cross (ICRC)
Washington Delegation
2100 Pennsylvania Ave. NW, Suite 5454, Washington, DC 20038
(202) 293-9430
Web site: www.icrc.org

Founded in 1863, the ICRC is an independent organization whose exclusive humanitarian mission is to protect the lives and dignity of victims of war and internal violence. It directs and coordinates international relief activities and promotes humanitarian law and principles. Its Web site includes the text of the Geneva Conventions, subsequent protocols, and articles and reports on recent issues related to its mission. ICRC publishes the journal *International Review of the Red Cross*, recent issues of which are available on its Web site.

Nuclear Age Peace Foundation
1187 Coast Village Rd., Suite 1, PMB 121, Santa Barbara, CA 93108-2794
(805) 965-3443 • fax: (805) 568-0466
Web site: www.wagingpeace.org

Founded in 1982, the Nuclear Age Peace Foundation, a nonprofit, nonpartisan international education and advocacy organization, initiates and supports worldwide efforts to abolish nuclear weapons, to strengthen international law and institutions, to use technology responsibly and sustainably, and to empower youth to create a more peaceful world. Its Web site has a searchable database of news, editorials, and articles, including "Terrorism and Nonviolence" and "The Iraq War and the Future of International Law."

Reason Foundation
3415 S. Sepulveda Blvd., Suite 400, Los Angeles, CA 90034
(310) 391-2245 • fax: (310) 391-4395
Web site: www.reason.org

The foundation promotes individual freedoms and free-market principles, and opposes U.S. interventionism in foreign affairs. Its publications include the monthly *Reason* magazine, recent issues of which are available at www.reason.com. The foundation's Web site, linked to the Reason Public Policy Institute at www.rppi.org, publishes online versions of institute articles and reports.

Resource Center for Nonviolence
515 Broadway, Santa Cruz, CA 95060
(831) 423-1626 • fax: (831) 423-8716
e-mail: information@rcnv.org • Web site: www.rcnv.org

The Resource Center for Nonviolence was founded in 1976 and promotes nonviolence as a force for personal and social change. The center provides speakers, workshops, leadership development, and nonviolence training programs. Its Web site publishes editorials, essays, news articles, and reports.

United for Peace and Justice (UFPJ)
PO Box 607, Times Square Station, New York, NY 10108
(212) 868-5545
Web site: www.unitedforpeace.org

UFPJ opposes preemptive wars of aggression and rejects any drive to expand U.S. control over other nations. It rejects the use of war and racism to concentrate power in the hands of the few. The UFPJ Web site publishes accounts of antiwar events, news articles, and essays.

United Nations Association of the United States of America
801 Second Ave., New York, NY 10017
(212) 907-1300 • fax: (212) 682-9185
e-mail: unahq@unausa.org • Web site: www.unausa.org

The association is a nonpartisan, nonprofit research organization dedicated to strengthening both the United Nations and U.S. participation in the UN council. Its publications include *Interdependent*, a quarterly magazine. Its Web site publishes press releases, annual reports, fact sheets, surveys, and articles, including "A Beacon in the Dark: The International Criminal Court."

Bibliography of Books

John B. Alexander — *Future War: Non-Lethal Weapons in Modern Warfare.* New York: St. Martin's Press, 1999.

Robert J. Art and Kenneth N. Waltz, eds. — *The Use of Force: Military Power and International Politics.* Lanham, MD: Rowman & Littlefield, 2004.

David P. Barash and Charles P. Webel — *Peace and Conflict Studies.* Thousand Oaks, CA: Sage, 2002.

Tarak Barkawi and Mark Laffey, eds. — *Democracy, Liberalism, and War: Rethinking the Democratic Peace Debate.* Boulder, CO: Lynne Rienner, 2001.

Omer Bartov — *Mirrors of Destruction: War, Genocide, and Modern Identity.* New York: Oxford University Press, 2000.

Michael V. Bhatia — *War and Intervention: Issues for Contemporary Peace Operations.* Bloomfield, CT: Kumarian Press, 2003.

Jeremy Black — *War in the New Century.* New York: Continuum, 2001.

Christopher Coker — *Humane Warfare.* New York: Routledge, 2001.

Christopher Coker — *Waging War Without Warriors?: The Changing Culture of Military Conflict.* Boulder, CO: Lynne Rienner, 2002.

Paul F. Diehl and Gary Goertz — *War and Peace in International Rivalry.* Ann Arbor: University of Michigan Press, 2000.

Brian E. Fogarty — *War, Peace, and the Social Order.* Boulder, CO: Westview Press, 2000.

George Friedman and Meredith Friedman — *The Future of War: Power, Technology, and American World Dominance in the Twenty-first Century.* New York: St. Martin's Press, 1998.

Melanie Greenberg — *Words over War: Mediation and Arbitration to Prevent Deadly Conflict.* Lanham, MD: Rowman & Littlefield, 2000.

Stacy Bergstrom Haldi — *Why Wars Widen: A Theory of Predation and Balancing.* Portland, OR: Frank Cass, 2003.

Robert E. Harkavy and Stephanie G. Neuman — *Warfare and the Third World.* New York: Palgrave, 2001.

Errol Anthony Henderson — *Democracy and War: The End of an Illusion?* Boulder, CO: Lynne Rienner, 2002.

Kelly M. Kadera — *The Power-Conflict Story: A Dynamic Model of Interstate Rivalry.* Ann Arbor: University of Michigan Press, 2001.

John Keegan	*War and Our World.* New York: Vintage, 2001.
Felix Knüpling	*Democracies and War: An Investigation of Theoretical Explanations.* Piscataway, NJ: Transaction, 2000.
John A. Lynn	*Battle: A History of Combat and Culture.* Boulder, CO: Westview Press, 2003.
Zeev Maoz and Azar Gat	*War in a Changing World.* Ann Arbor: University of Michigan Press, 2001.
Colin McInnes	*Spectator-Sport War: The West and Contemporary Conflict.* Boulder, CO: Lynne Rienner, 2002.
John Norton Moore	*Solving the War Puzzle: Beyond the Democratic Peace.* Durham, NC: Carolina Academic Press, 2004.
Hanna Newcombe	*War, Peace, and Weapons.* Dundas, ON: Peace Research Institute, 2001.
Dan Reiter	*Democracies at War.* Princeton, NJ: Princeton University Press, 2002.
Jonathan Schell	*The Unconquerable World: Power, Nonviolence, and the Will of the People.* New York: Metropolitan, 2003.
Martin Shaw	*War and Genocide: Organized Killing in Modern Society.* Cambridge, UK: Polity Press, 2003.
Brian Steed	*Armed Conflict: The Lessons of Modern Warfare.* New York: Ballantine, 2003.
John George Stoessinger	*Why Nations Go to War.* Belmont, CA: Thomson/Wadsworth, 2001.
John A. Vasquez	*What Do We Know About War?* Lanham, MD: Rowman & Littlefield, 2000.

Index

Abrams, Elliot, 107
Abu Ghraib prison, 116
Afghanistan, 133, 186
Agenda for Peace (Boutros-Ghali), 166
American Conservative (magazine), 97
Annan, Kofi, 202, 203
Arab-Israeli War (1948–1949), 45, 66
Arafat, Yasser, 48, 185
Asia, financial meltdown in, 29–30
Asmal, Kader, 16–17
Augustine, Saint, 67, 101
Ayala, Balthazar, 149
Ayn Rand Institute, 45, 129, 132

Baker, James, 144
Bandow, Doug, 61
Begin, Menachem, 94
Bernstein, Andrew, 45
Berry, Wendell, 71
Bhikkhu, Santikaro, 73
Biden, Joseph, 204
bin Laden, Osama, 39, 46, 126
Blix, Hans, 175
Bobbitt, Philip, 130
Borger, Julian, 42
Bosnian War (1992–1994), 209, 217–18
  UN Tribunal for crimes committed in, 161–62
Boudin, Louis, 213
Boutros-Ghali, Boutros, 166
Bugnion, François, 141
Bush, George H.W., 84
Bush, George W., 169, 174
  decision to invade Iraq and, 63–64
  position of, on International Criminal Court, 157
  on preemption policy, 86, 91, 92
Bush administration, 144
  Guantánamo Bay detainees and, 120
  preemptive war policy of, 138, 201
    leads to Iraq invasion, 90
    precedents for, 84–85
    risks of, 95–97
    violates UN Charter, 81, 91
Byers, Michael, 93, 136
Byrd, Robert, 117

Camus, Albert, 67
Canada, 30
capitalism
  brought longest period of peace, 48
  as economic warfare, 76–77
  leads to war, 38–44
    con, 45–48
      risk-taking and, 43
Carey, George, 63
Carnegie, Andrew, 161
Carnegie Commission on Preventing Deadly Conflict, 201
Carnell, Brian, 128
Caroline case (1837), 84–85
Carpenter, Ted Galen, 167
Carroll, Vincent, 23
Carter, Jimmy, 46
Casey, Lee A., 146
Cato the Elder, 93
cease-fires, 215
Central Intelligence Agency (CIA), 36
Cheney, Dick, 41, 177
Christianity
  nonviolent ethic of, 26
  wars fought over, 24–25
Churchill, Winston, 82
church-state separation, 22
City of God (Augustine), 101
civilians
  casualties among, in World War II, 178
  objectivist view on targeting of, 129
  reevaluation of prohibition against targeting, 140–41
  should not be targeted to spare combatants, 128–31
    con, 132–35
Civil War (1861–1865), 75
Classical Liberals, 206
  free trade position of, 207
Clinton, Bill, 85, 169
  position of, on International Criminal Court, 157
Cold War
  peace dividend from ending of, 39
  Security Council deadlocks during, 82
combatants
  civilians should not be targeted to spare, 128–31
    con, 132–35
  unlawful, 120-21
communism, 27
comparative advantage, theory of, 206–207
Congress, U.S., 60–61
Constitution, U.S., 60
Cooper, Marc, 112
corporations, relationship between militaries and, 32–33
Covenant of the League of Nations (1919), 81

Cromwell, Oliver, 25
Crusades, 24, 25
Cuban Missile Crisis (1962), 83, 86

Dalton, Andrew, 129, 131
Dawkins, Richard, 24
Declaration of Independence, 60
democratic peace theory, origin of, 191
Demosthenes, 188
developing world
  globalization has expanded
    political/civil freedoms in, 35–36
  military spending in, 31
  wars in, 29
Dickinson, Emily, 21
Djinjic, Zoran, 161
Dresden (Germany), bombing of,
  129–30, 134
Dunant, Henri, 137
Dworkin, Anthony, 116

Ebeling, Richard M., 205
Ehrenreich, Barbara, 53
Eisenhower, Dwight D., 209
Elshtain, Jean Bethke, 67, 68
England. *See* United Kingdom
environmental destruction
  Geneva Convention on, 13–14
  in Gulf War, 12
Environmental Modification
  Convention (ENMOD), 14
Epstein, Alex, 49
Ex parte Quirin (1942), 125

Falk, Richard, 111
Fanton, Jonathan F., 156
free trade
  Classical Liberals' position on, 206,
    207
  policies could not prevent World
    War I, 211–12
  promotion of, will avoid war, 205–13
Friedman, Thomas, 32
Friends Committee on National
  Legislation, 200

Gandhi, Mohandas, 73
Geneva Convention (1949), 151
  on environmental destruction in
    warfare, 13–14
  Guantánamo Bay detainees and, 120,
    139
  Protocol I Additional, 147
    excerpts from, 150
    perils of, 152–53
  on treatment of prisoners of war, 116
    applies only to lawful combatants,
      125–26

Geneva law, on armed conflict, 164
genocide, Rwandan, 162
George III (king of England), 60
George VI (king of England), 174
Ghate, Onkar, 132
Glennon, Michael J., 80
globalization
  of conflicting religions, 20–21
  promotes wars, 28–33
    con, 34–37
Global Justice Ecology Project, 31
Global Partnership for the Prevention
  of Armed Conflict, 202
Gonzales, Alberto, 139
Goure, Daniel, 174
Great Britain. *See* United Kingdom
Green Party of Great Britain, 38
Gregory VIII (pope), 25
Gregory XIII (pope), 25
Griswold, Daniel T., 34
Grossman, Dave, 54
Guantánamo Bay detainees, 120, 122,
  139
Guardian (newspaper), 42
Gulf War Syndrome, 178–79

Hague law, on armed conflict, 145,
  164
Hague tribunal, on Rwandan genocide,
  162
Halliburton, 41–42
Hanson, Victor Davis, 56, 182
Harris, Arthur, 130
Harris, Eric, 27
Harvey, Paul, 24
Haught, James A., 20
Heraclitus, 183
Heritage Foundation, 36
Hiroshima, bombing of, 129–30, 134
Hitler, Adolf, 47
Ho Chi Minh, 48
Holy Trinity of Doncaster, 26
Homer, 147
Hoon, Geoff, 143–44
Houweling, Henk, 56
Human Rights Watch, 120
Hume, David, 207
Hussein, Saddam, 12, 46, 158, 183
  placed Iraqi citizens in harm's way,
    152–53

Ignatieff, Michael, 116–17
Ikenberry, G. John, 95, 97
Iliad, The (Homer), 147
imperialism, 65
income, per capita, 36
Inder, Claire, 13
Indo-Chinese War (1962), 196

Institute for American Values, 99
International Committee of the Red
    Cross (ICRC), 151
International Court of Justice (ICJ),
    161
International Criminal Court (ICC)
    concept of, 158
    ratification of treaty establishing,
        157, 163
    safeguards in, 159, 168
    scope of, 167–68
    U.S. should join, to pursue war
        crimes, 156–59
        con, 160–70
international laws
    Martens Clause and, 145
    U.S. should reject strict enforcement
        of, 146–55
        con, 136–45
    see also Geneva Convention
International Monetary Fund (IMF),
    30
interventionism, rise of, 210–11
Iraq
    childhood deaths from sanctions on,
        179
    1981 Israeli attack on, 94–95
    2003 invasion of, 60, 144–45
        just-war tradition and, 69
        UN fails to authorize, 154, 175
    see also Persian Gulf War
Islamicism, 103–104
Israel, 45, 66, 183
    1981 attack on Iraq by, 94–95

James, William, 65
jingoism, 193
Johnson, Douglas A., 116
Johnson, James Turner, 26
Johnson, Lyndon, 95, 193
Jones, Jenny, 39
jus ad bellum, 137
    Bush doctrine of preemptive war
        and, 138
jus in bello, 137
    efforts to reform, 151–52
Just War Against Terror: The Burden of
    American Power in a Violent World
    (Elshtain), 67
just-war tradition, 26, 68
    principles of, 101–102
    targeting of civilians and, 131

Kant, Immanuel, 191, 192
Katz, Mark N., 185
Keating, Raymond J., 85
Kegley, Charles W., Jr., 89
Keller, Bill, 95, 97

Kellogg-Briand Peace Pact (1928), 81,
    90
Kennedy, Andrew, 16
Kennedy, Edward M., 117
Kennedy, John F., 85
Keynes, John, 41
King, Martin Luther, Jr., 73
Klebold, Dylan, 27
Korean War (1950–1953), public
    support for, 193
Kosovo War (1999), 215
    indirect targeting of civilians in,
        140–41
Kurds, 27
Kuwait. See Persian Gulf War

Laghi, Pio, 63–64
League of Nations. See Covenant of
    the League of Nations
Le Duc Tho, 48
liberalism, role in avoiding war,
    194–95
Libertarian Watch (magazine), 129
Libya, U.S. attack on, 83
    consequences of, 107–108
Lincoln, Abraham, 74
    on danger of war powers in hands of
        rulers, 60
Locke, John, 192
Loconte, Joseph, 117
London Review of Books, The, 93
Luttwak, Edward N., 214

Manuel, Trevor, 31
Maoz, Zeev, 192
Martens Clause, 145
Martin, David, 27
Marx, Karl, 56
Mbeki, Thabo, 40
McCarthy, Rory, 42
McCollum, Sean, 60
McKinley, William, 193
McVeigh, Timothy, 109
Megrahi, Abdelbaset Ali Mohmed al,
    162
militarism, globalization contributes
    to, 29
military strategy, environmental
    destruction as, 12–14
Mill, John Stuart, 192
Milosevic, Slobodan, 47, 161, 167
Mises, Ludwig von, 209–10, 211
missile defense, 187
Muhammad (the prophet), 104
Morris, Dick, 111

Nagasaki, bombing of, 130, 134
nationalism, 27

National Security Strategy of the United States (NSS), 91
National Strategy to Combat Weapons of Mass Destruction, 144
Nazism, 27
Neill, Stephen, 25
New Yorker (magazine), 139
nongovernmental organizations (NGOs), 220–22
  peaceful prevention efforts by, 202
Norman, Fredrik, 129
North Atlantic Treaty Organization (NATO), 215
Nuclear Posture Review, 143
Nye, Joseph, 63

"Of the Jealousy of Trade" (Hume), 207
Oliver, Charles, 129
On Killing: The Psychological Cost of Learning to Kill in War and Society (Grossman), 54
Operation Iraqi Freedom. *See* Iraq, 2003 invasion of
Ottawa anti-landmine convention (1997), 147

pacifism
  in Christian tradition, 26
  escalates wars, 49–52
Paine, Thomas, 192
Passy, Frederic, 207, 208
peace enforcement, 166
Pearl Harbor attack (1941), 94
Pernoud, Regine, 27
Perpetual Peace (Kant), 191
Persian Gulf War (1991), 196–97, 209
  casualties of, 137, 178–79
  environmental destruction from, 12
  indirect targeting of civilians in, 140
  as war of self-defense, 127
Philippine-American War (1899–1902), 198
Pitts, John, 126
Plague, The (Camus), 67
Pol Pot, 47, 158
Polybius, 94
Powell, Colin, 63, 103
  pushes for Geneva Convention recognition for Taliban prisoners, 122
Power, Jonathan, 203
prisoners of war
  detainees in war on terror should be treated as, 118–23
    con, 124–27
  Geneva Convention on treatment of, 116

protectionism, rise of, 210–11

el-Qaddafi, Muammar, 107, 162
al-Qaeda, 103, 109, 184
  members of, are unlawful combatants, 126
  see also Guantánamo Bay detainees
Qur'an (Koran), 103, 104

Rand, Ayn, 47, 48
Ray, James Lee, 192
Raymond, Gregory A., 89
Read, Piers Paul, 25
Reagan, Ronald, 95
refugee camps, 219–20
religious conflicts, cause war, 18–22
  con, 23–27
Report on the Prevention of Armed Conflict (UN Secretary General), 201
Responsibility to Protect (International Commission on Intervention and State Sovereignty), 201
Rights of Man (Paine), 192
Rivkin, David B., 146
Rome, ancient
  environmental destruction as tactic of, 93–94
  Third Punic War and, 93–94
Roosevelt, Franklin D., 94
"Roots of War, The" (Rand), 47
Rotunda, Ronald D., 124
Royal United Services Institute for Defence Studies (RUSI), 16–17
Rummel, R.J., 190
Rumsfeld, Donald, 177
  on status of Guantánamo Bay detainees, 119, 123, 139
Russett, Bruce, 192

Saint Bartholomew's Day Massacre, 25
Sane, Pierre, 203
Saving Lives, Enriching Life: Freedom as a Right and a Moral Good (Rummel), 190
Schell, Jonathan, 64, 65, 66, 69
School of the Americas, 109
Schraeder, Paul, 97
secularism, possibility of, 21–22
self-defense
  right of, in UN Charter, 81–82
  wars of, do not need to be declared, 127
Seligman, Carole, 42
September 11 attacks, 19, 46, 102–103, 135
  were aimed at corporate America, 39
  were the consequences of pacifism, 50–51

Shapiro, Bruce, 118
Sharon, Ariel, 185
Sherman, William Tecumseh, 12
Shield of Achilles, The (Bobbitt), 130
Six-Day War (1967), 66
Smeal, Eleanor, 112
Smith, Adam, 192, 213
Solferino, Battle of, 137
Somme, Battle of the, 198
Soros, George, 110
South Africa, military expansion in,
    31–32, 40
Sowell, Thomas, 51
space, militarization of, 32
Spanish-American War (1898–1899),
    198
    public support for, 193
Spencer, Dane, 176
Stalin, Joseph, 47
Staples, Steven, 28
statism, 47
Stephens, Patrick, 134
Strozier, Charles B., 116

Taliban, 46, 109, 112, 126, 139
    see also Guantánamo Bay detainees
Taylor, Stuart, 130
terrorism. *See* war on terror
Themistocles, 188
Third Punic War, 93–94
third world. *See* developing world
Thirty Years' War (1618–1648), 98
Tonkin Gulf Resolution (1964), 193
torture, 116–17
Tosteson, Daniel C., 18
Townsend, Mark, 16
Truman, Harry, 130, 193
Twain, Mark, 16, 20

*Unconquerable World: Power,
    Nonviolence, and the Will of the People*
    (Schell), 64–65
United Kingdom
    pre–World War I trade policy of,
        211–12
    subsidy of arms industry in, 40
    World War I and foreign policy of,
        198
United Nations, 174–75
    Charter
        Bush's preemptive war policy
            violates, 81, 91
        use-of-force rules of, have been
            ignored, 88
    Human Development Report (1999),
        29
    interventions in wars by, 215
    peacekeepers of, are ineffectual,

216–18
    Relief and Works Agency
        (UNRWA), 219–20
    resolution enhancing effectiveness of,
        in addressing conflict, 203
    Tribunal for the former Yugoslavia,
        161–62
United States
    military budget of, 31
    should join International Criminal
        Court to pursue war crimes,
        156–59
        con, 160–70
    should reject strict international laws
        of war, 146–55
        con, 136–45
    Space Command, 32
    war-making authority in, 60–61, 127
Urban II (pope), 25

Vidal, Gore, 24
Vietnam War (1964–1973), 48
    designation of unlawful combatants
        in, 121
    effects of civilian casualties in, 131
    environmental destruction from, 13

Wall Street Journal (newspaper), 36
war
    can be prevented, 176–80
        con, 182–89
    dictatorial regimes cause, 46–47
    earliest evidence of, 54
    fostering democracy worldwide will
        prevent, 190–99
    is sometimes justified to maintain
        peace and freedom, 62–70
        con, 71–79
    leads to lasting peace, 214–22
    peaceful intervention can prevent,
        200–204
    preemptive, may be justified, 80–88
        con, 89–98
    severity of, 196–97
    warlike societies perpetuate, 53–57
warfare
    modern, contradictions of, 72–73
    policing model of, 148–49
war on terror
    civilians may legitimately be targeted
        in, 133
    detainees in, should be treated as
        prisoners of war, 118–23
        con, 124–27
    is justified, 99–105
        con, 106–12
War Powers Resolution (1973), 61
war profiteering, 42

water resources, as cause of future
  wars, 16–17
weapons, banning of inhumane, 143
Webster, Daniel, 84–85
Wedgwood, Ruth, 160
Weigel, George, 62
Weinstein, James, 67
Wills, Gary, 24
Wilson, Woodrow, 95
Wise, Tim, 106
World Bank, 36
World Trade Organization (WTO), 30
World War I (1914–1918), 55–56, 196,
  208

effects of, on British foreign policy,
  198
free trade policies could not prevent,
  211–12
World War II (1939–1945), 196,
  208–209
  civilian casualties of, 178
  German and Soviet deaths in, 197
  military tribunals following, 125
  targeting of civilians in, 134
  war profiteering in, 42

Yugoslavia, UN Tribunal and, 161–62